Macroeconomics: Theory, Models & Poli

Douglas Curtis and Ian Irvine

End of Chapter Exercises & Solutions

Version 2015 — **Revision A**

The content in this version is differentiated from the 2014 version solely by minor editorial adjustments.

lyryx
advancing learning

LYRYX WITH OPEN TEXTS

The form of this book is completely new to the Canadian market. As authors we have many years of experience in hard copy book publishing with a major international publisher. This time we are publishing an **open text** in collaboration with Lyryx Learning, supporting open content as part of their *Lyryx with Open Texts* products & services.

While there is no requirement that users of the book do anything more than download the pdf files and use them for non-profit educational purposes, the texts are aligned with *Lyryx with Open Texts* products and services offering the following benefits.

OPEN TEXT

The text can be downloaded in electronic format, printed, and can be distributed to students at no cost. Instructors who adopt *Lyryx with Open Texts* may obtain the relevant original text files from the authors if the instructors decide they wish to amplify certain sections for their own students. In collaboration with the authors, Lyryx will also adapt the content and provide custom editions for specific courses.

ONLINE ASSESSMENT

Lyryx has developed corresponding *formative* online assessment for homework and quizzes. These are genuine questions for the subject and adapted to the content. Student answers are carefully analyzed by the system and personalized feedback is immediately provided to help students improve on their work. Lyryx provides all the tools required to manage your online assessment including student grade reports and student performance statistics.

INSTRUCTOR SUPPLEMENTS

A number of resources are available, including a full set of slides for instructors and students. These are available in their original format, and consequently can be further adapted by instructors. An *Exam Builder* tool is also available allowing instructors to easily create paper quizzes and exams.

SUPPORT

Lyryx provides all of the support you and your students need! Starting from the course preparation time to beyond the end of the course, the Lyryx staff is available 7 days/week to provide assistance. This may include adapting the text, managing multiple sections of the course, providing course supplements, as well as timely assistance to students with registration, navigation, and daily organization.

Contact Lyryx!
info@lyryx.com

EXERCISES FOR CHAPTER 1

Exercise 1.1. An economy has 100 workers. Each one can produce four cakes or three shirts, regardless of the number of other individuals producing each good. Assuming all workers are employed, draw the *PPF* for this economy, with cakes on the vertical axis and shirts on the horizontal axis.

   (a) How many cakes can be produced in this economy when all the workers are cooking?

   (b) How many shirts can be produced in this economy when all the workers are sewing?

   (c) Join these points with a straight line; this is the *PPF*.

   (d) Label the inefficient and unattainable regions on the diagram.

Exercise 1.2. In the table below are listed a series of points that define an economy's production possibility frontier for goods Y and X.

Y	1000	900	800	700	600	500	400	300	200	100	0
X	0	1600	2500	3300	4000	4600	5100	5500	5750	5900	6000

   (a) Plot these points to scale, on graph paper, or with the help of a spreadsheet.

   (b) Given the shape of this *PPF* is the economy made up of individuals who are similar or different in their production capabilities?

   (c) What is the opportunity cost of producing 100 more Y at the combination $(X = 5500, Y = 300)$.

   (d) Suppose next there is technological change so that at every output level of good Y the economy can produce 20 percent more X. Compute the co-ordinates for the new economy and plot the new *PPF*.

Exercise 1.3. Using the *PPF* that you have graphed using the data in Exercise 1.2, determine if the following combinations are attainable or not: $(X = 3000, Y = 720)$, $(X = 4800, Y = 480)$.

Exercise 1.4. You and your partner are highly efficient people. You can earn $50 per hour in the workplace; your partner can earn $60 per hour.

(a) What is the opportunity cost of one hour of leisure for you?

(b) What is the opportunity cost of one hour of leisure for your partner?

(c) Now draw the *PPF* for yourself where hours of leisure is on the horizontal axis and income in dollars is on the vertical axis. You can assume that you have 12 hours of time each day to allocate to work (income generation) or leisure.

(d) Draw the *PPF* for your partner.

(e) If there is no domestic cleaning service in your area, which of you should do the housework, assuming that you are equally efficient at housework?

Exercise 1.5. Louis and Carrie Anne are students who have set up a summer business in their neighbourhood. They cut lawns and clean cars. Louis is particularly efficient at cutting the grass – he requires one hour to cut a typical lawn, while Carrie Anne needs one and one half hours. In contrast, Carrie Anne can wash a car in a half hour, while Louis requires three quarters of an hour.

(a) If they decide to specialize in the tasks, who should cut the grass and who should wash cars?

(b) If they each work a twelve hour day, how many lawns can they cut and how many cars can they wash if they specialize in performing the work?

Exercise 1.6. In Exercise 1.5, illustrate the *PPF* for each individual where lawns are on the horizontal axis and car washes on the vertical axis. Carefully label the intercepts. Then construct the economy-wide *PPF* using this information.

Exercise 1.7. Continuing with the same data set, suppose Carrie Anne's productivity improves so that she can now cut grass as efficiently as Louis; that is, she can cut grass in one hour, and can still wash a car in one half of an hour.

(a) In a new diagram draw the *PPF* for each individual.

(b) In this case does specialization matter if they are to be as productive as possible as a team?

(c) Draw the new *PPF* for the whole economy, labelling the intercepts and kink point coordinates.

Exercise 1.8. Using the economy-wide *PPF* you have constructed in Exercise 1.7, consider the impact of technological change in the economy. The tools used by Louis and Carrie Anne to cut grass and wash cars increase the efficiency of each worker by a whopping 25%. Illustrate graphically how this impacts the aggregate *PPF* and compute the three new sets of coordinates.

Exercise 1.9. Going back to the simple *PPF* plotted for Exercise 1.1 where each of 100 workers can produce either four cakes or three shirts, suppose a recession reduces demand for the outputs to 220 cakes and 129 shirts.

(a) Plot this combination of outputs in the diagram that also shows the *PPF*.

(b) How many workers are needed to produce this output of cakes and shirts?

(c) What percentage of the 100 worker labour force is unemployed?

EXERCISES FOR CHAPTER 2

Exercise 2.1. An examination of a country's recent international trade flows yields the data in the table below.

Year	National Income ($b)	Imports ($b)
2011	1,500	550
2012	1,575	573
2013	1,701	610
2014	1,531	560
2015	1,638	591

(a) Based on an examination of these data do you think the national income and imports are not related, positively related, or negatively related?

(b) Draw a simple two dimensional line diagram to illustrate your view of the import/income relationship. Measure income on the horizontal axis and imports on the vertical axis.

Exercise 2.2. The average price of a medium coffee at *Wakeup Coffee Shop* in each of the past ten years is given in the table below.

2005	2006	2007	2008	2009	2010	2011	2012	2013	2014
$1.05	$1.10	$1.14	$1.20	$1.25	$1.25	$1.33	$1.35	$1.45	$1.49

(a) Construct an annual 'coffee price index' for the 2005 time period using 2006 as the base year.

(b) Based on your price index, what was the percentage change in the price of a medium coffee from 2006 to 2013?

(c) Based on your index, what was the average annual percentage change in the price of coffee from 2010 to 2013?

Exercise 2.3. The table below gives unemployment rates for big cities and the rest of the country. Two-thirds of the population lives in the big cities, and one-third in other areas. Construct a national unemployment index, using the year 2000 as the base.

Unemployment (%)		
Year	Big Cities	Other Areas
2007	5	7
2008	7	10
2009	8	9
2010	10	12
2011	9	11

Exercise 2.4. The prices in the following table below are for three components in a typical consumer's budget: transportation, rent, and food. You must construct an aggregate price index based on these three components on the assumption that rent accounts for 55 percent of the weight in this index, food for 35 percent, and transport for 10 percent. You should start by computing an index for each component, using year 1 as the base period.

	Year 1	Year 2	Year 3	Year 4	Year 5
Transport $	70	70	75	75	75
Rent $	1000	1000	1100	1120	1150
Food $	600	620	610	640	660

Exercise 2.5. The price of carrots per kilogram is given in the table below for several years, as is the corresponding CPI.

	2000	2002	2004	2006	2008	2010
Nominal						
Carrot Price $	2.60	2.90	3.30	3.30	3.10	3.00
CPI	110	112	115	117	120	124

(a) Compute a nominal price index for carrots using 2000 as the base period.

(b) Re-compute the CPI using 2000 as the base year.

(c) Construct a real price index for carrots.

Exercise 2.6. The following table shows hypothetical consumption spending by households and income of households in billions of dollars.

Year	Income	Consumption
2006	476	434
2007	482	447
2008	495	454
2009	505	471
2010	525	489
2011	539	509
2012	550	530
2013	567	548

(a) Plot the scatter diagram with consumption on the vertical axis and income on the horizontal axis.

(b) Fit a line through these points.

(c) Does the line indicate that these two variables are related to each other?

(d) How would you describe the *causal relationship* between income and consumption?

Exercise 2.7. Using the data from Exercise 2.6, compute the percentage change in consumption and the percentage change in income for each pair of adjoining years between 2006 and 2013.

Exercise 2.8. You are told that the relationship between two variables, X and Y, has the form $Y = 10 + 2X$. By trying different values for X you can obtain the corresponding predicted value for Y (e.g., if $X = 3$, then $Y = 10 + 2 \times 3 = 16$). For values of X between 0 and 12, compute the matching value of Y and plot the scatter diagram.

Exercise 2.9. Perform the same exercise as in Exercise 2.8, but use the formula $Y = 10 - 0.5X$. What do you notice about the slope of the relationship?

Exercise 2.10. For the data below, plot a scatter diagram with variable Y on the vertical axis and variable X on the horizontal axis.

Y	40	33	29	56	81	19	20
X	5	7	9	3	1	11	10

(a) Is the relationship between the variables positive or negative?

(b) Do you think that a linear or non-linear line better describes the relationship?

EXERCISES FOR CHAPTER 3

Exercise 3.1. Supply and demand data for concerts are shown below.

Price	$20	$24	$28	$32	$36	$40
Quantity demanded	10	9	8	7	6	5
Quantity supplied	1	3	5	7	9	11

(a) Plot the supply and demand curves to scale and establish the equilibrium price and quantity.

(b) What is the excess supply or demand when price is $24? When price is $36?

(c) Describe the market adjustments in price induced by these two prices.

(d) The functions underlying the example in the table are linear and can be presented as $P = 18 + 2Q$ (supply) and $P = 60 - 4Q$ (demand). Solve the two equations for the equilibrium price and quantity values.

Exercise 3.2. Illustrate in a supply/demand diagram, by shifting the demand curve appropriately, the effect on the demand for flights between Calgary and Winnipeg as a result of:

(a) Increasing the annual government subsidy to *Via Rail*.

(b) Improving the Trans-Canada highway between the two cities.

(c) The arrival of a new budget airline on the scene.

Exercise 3.3. A new trend in U.S. high schools is the widespread use of chewing tobacco. A recent survey indicates that 15 percent of males in upper grades now use it – a figure not far below the use rate for cigarettes. Apparently this development came about in response to the widespread implementation by schools of regulations that forbade cigarette smoking on and around school property. Draw a supply-demand equilibrium for each of the cigarette and chewing tobacco markets before and after the introduction of the regulations.

Exercise 3.4. In Exercise 3.1, suppose there is a simultaneous shift in supply and demand caused by an improvement in technology and a growth in incomes. The technological improvement is represented by a lower supply curve: $P = 10 + 2Q$. The higher incomes boost demand to $P = 76 - 4Q$.

(a) Draw the new supply and demand curves on a diagram and compare them with the pre-change curves.

(b) Equate the new supply and demand functions and solve for the new equilibrium price and quantity.

Exercise 3.5. The market for labour can be described by two linear equations. Demand is given by $P = 170 - (1/6)Q$, and supply is given by $P = 50 + (1/3)Q$, where Q is the quantity of labour and P is the price of labour – the wage rate.

(a) Graph the functions and find the equilibrium price and quantity by equating demand and supply.

(b) Suppose a price ceiling is established by the government at a price of $120. This price is below the equilibrium price that you have obtained in part a. Calculate the amount that would be demanded and supplied and then calculate the excess demand.

Exercise 3.6. In Exercise 3.5, suppose that the supply and demand describe an agricultural market rather than a labour market, and the government implements a price floor of $140. This is greater than the equilibrium price.

(a) Estimate the quantity supplied and the quantity demanded at this price, and calculate the excess supply.

(b) Suppose the government instead chose to maintain a price of $140 by implementing a system of quotas. What quantity of quotas should the government make available to the suppliers?

Exercise 3.7. In Exercise 3.6, suppose that, at the minimum price, the government buys up all of the supply that is not demanded, and exports it at a price of $80 per unit. Compute the cost to the government of this operation.

Exercise 3.8. Let us sum two demand curves to obtain a 'market' demand curve. We will suppose there are just two buyers in the market. The two demands are defined by: $P = 42 - (1/3)Q$ and $P = 42 - (1/2)Q$.

(a) Draw the demands (approximately to scale) and label the intercepts on both the price and quantity axes.

(b) Determine how much would be purchased at prices $10, $20, and $30.

Exercise 3.9. In Exercise 3.8 the demand curves had the same price intercept. Suppose instead that the first demand curve is given by $P = 36 - (1/3)Q$ and the second is unchanged. Graph these curves and illustrate the market demand curve.

Exercise 3.10. Here is an example of a demand curve that is not linear: $P = 5 - 0.2\sqrt{Q}$. The final term here is the square root of Q.

(a) Draw this function on a graph and label the intercepts. You will see that the price intercept is easily obtained. Can you obtain the quantity intercept where $P = 0$?

(b) To verify that the shape of your function is correct you can plot this demand curve in a spreadsheet.

(c) If the supply curve in this market is given simply by $P = 2$, what is the equilibrium quantity traded?

Exercise 3.11. The football stadium of the University of the North West Territories has 30 seats. The demand for tickets is given by $P = 36 - (1/2)Q$, where Q is the number of ticket-buying fans.

(a) At the equilibrium admission price how much revenue comes in from ticket sales for each game?

(b) A local fan is offering to install 6 more seats at no cost to the University. Compute the price that would be charged with this new supply and compute the revenue that would accrue each game. Should the University accept the offer to install the seats?

(c) Redo part (b) of this question, assuming that the initial number of seats is 40, and the University has the option to increase capacity to 46 at no cost to itself. Should the University accept the offer in this case?

Exercise 3.12. Suppose farm workers in Mexico are successful in obtaining a substantial wage increase. Illustrate the effect of this on the price of lettuce in the Canadian winter.

EXERCISES FOR CHAPTER 4

Exercise 4.1.

You have the following annual data for an economy:

Year	Real GDP (2002 $)	Consumer Price Index (2002=100)	Labour Force	Employment
2010	1,282	109.1	17.593	16.537
2011	1,307	111.9	17,857	16.696
2012	1,288	138.9	18.125	16.856

(a) What was the rate of growth of real GDP from 2010 to 2011, and 2011 to 2012?

(b) What was the rate of inflation in 2011 and in 2012?

(c) What were the rates of growth of the labour force and employment from 2010 to 2011, and 2011 to 2012?

(d) What happened to the unemployment rate between 2010 and 2011, and between 2011 and 2012?

Exercise 4.2. Suppose the economy represented by the table in Exercise 4.1 above had a population of 27.885 thousand in 2011.

(a) What were the participation and employment rates in the economy in those years?

(b) Suppose a mild recession in that year discouraged some unemployed workers and they stop looking for work. As a result the participation rate fell to 64.5 per cent. How would the unemployment rate and the employment rate be affected? Why?

Exercise 4.3. If brewers buy barley and hops from agricultural producers, natural gas to fire their brew kettles from gas companies and bottles from glass manufacturers as in the following table, what is the value added of the brewing industry?If brewers also wholesale some of their output to pubs, is that output counted in GDP? Explain your answer.

Costs (Millions of Current $) of:			
Brewery Retail Sales	**Barley and Hops**	**Natural Gas**	**Bottles**
1000	350	125	150

Exercise 4.4. The economy has two main industries. One produces services and the other produces goods. The services industries produce services for households and businesses with a total market value of $10,000. The goods industries produce goods for the use of both households and businesses with a total market value of $5,000. The service industries spend $1000 on computers and paper and envelopes supplied by the goods industries. The goods industries spend $1000 to buy financial, insurance, advertising and custodial supplied by the service industries. Explain how you measure nominal GDP in this economy and the value of output you find?

Exercise 4.5. Suppose you are given the following data on incomes and expenditures for the economy of Westland, in current prices for factors of production and outputs.

Consumption expenditures	2500
Employment income	2800
Government expenditure	800
Net indirect taxes	150
Exports	1200
Business income	700
Capital consumption allowance	200
Investment expenditure	600
Imports	2200
Investment income	150

(a) What is the value of nominal GDP measured by expenditures?

(b) What is net domestic income?

(c) What is the value of nominal GDP measured by the income approach?

Exercise 4.6. Suppose GDP is $2,000, consumption expenditure is $1,700, government expenditure is $50, and net exports are $40.

(a) What is business investment expenditure?

(b) If exports are $350, what are imports?

(c) If the capital consumption allowance for depreciation is $130 and net indirect taxes are $100, what is net domestic income?

(d) In this example, net exports are positive. Could they be negative?

Exercise 4.7. Consider the following information about a hypothetical economy:

Year	Nominal GDP (Billion $)	GDP Deflator (2000=100)	Population (Millions)
2012	750	104.0	25.0
2013	825	112.0	30.0

(a) Calculate the growth (percentage change) in nominal GDP from 2012 to 2013.

(b) What was real GDP in 2007 and 2008? How much did real GDP grow?

(c) If changes in the standard of living can be measured by changes in real per capita GDP, did growth in nominal and real GDP raise the standard of living in this economy from 2012 to 2013?

(d) Explain the reasons for the change in standard of living that you have found.

EXERCISES FOR CHAPTER 5

Exercise 5.1. Suppose we have the following information for an economy:

GDP Deflator	Planned Aggregate Expenditure	Planned Aggregate Output
90	550	150
100	500	300
110	450	450
120	400	600
130	350	750

(a) Plot the AD and AS curves in a carefully labeled diagram.

(b) What are the short-run equilibrium values of real GDP and the price level?

Exercise 5.2. Suppose we learn that potential output is 500 for the economy in Exercise 5.1.

(a) Add a line to your diagram for Exercise 5.1 to illustrate potential GDP.

(b) What is the size of any output gap you see in the diagram?

(c) What is the size and sign of the output gap?

Exercise 5.3. Potential GDP is determined by the size of the labour force, the stock of capital and the state of technology used in the production process. Assume the labour force grows over time, and research and development lead to improvements in technology, and productivity. Use an AD/AS diagram to illustrate potential GDP both before and after the growth in labour force and the improvement in technology.

Exercise 5.4. Consider an economy described by the following: AD: $Y = 2250 - 10P$, AS: $P = 125 + 0.1Y$.

(a) What are the short run equilibrium values for real GDP and the price level?

(b) Assume potential output is 500 and draw an AD/AS/Y_P diagram to show the initial short run equilibrium real GDP, price level and potential output.

(c) Changes in international market conditions drive up prices for crude oil and base metals. Increased production costs driven by these higher input prices raise the general price level by 5 at every level of output. Write the equation of the new AS curve. What are the new short run equilibrium real GDP and price level?

(d) Draw the new AS curve in your diagram for b). What is the size of the output gap?

Exercise 5.5. Growth in potential output is determined by growth in the labour force and growth in labour productivity. Suppose the labour force grows by 1.5 percent a year and labour productivity, based on increased capital and improved technology, grows by 1.0 percent a year.

(a) What is the annual growth in potential output?

(b) Illustrate the growth in potential output in an AD/AS diagram.

(c) Aggregate demand is not changed by the change in potential output. Indicate any output gap caused by the change in potential output.

Exercise 5.6. Suppose we have the following data for an economy:

Year	Potential Output (billions 2002$)	Real GDP (billions 2002$)
2006	1,038	1,017
2007	1,069	1,030
2008	1,101	1,101
2009	1,134	1,160
2010	1,168	1,139
2011	1,203	1,130
2012	1,240	1,187
2013	1,277	1,163

Calculate the output gap for each year in this economy. Plot the output gap in a time series diagram. Date the timing of the phases of any business cycles you see in your plot of the output gap.

Exercise 5.7. Suppose employment in the economy is proportional to output based on the output function $Y = 100N$, where N is employment in person years. If a recessionary gap reduced output (Y) by 1.0 percent what change in employment would result?

EXERCISES FOR CHAPTER 6

Exercise 6.1. Suppose that in an economy with no government the consumption function is: $C = 50 + 0.75Y$.

(a) Draw a diagram showing the consumption function, and indicate the level of consumption expenditure when income is 150.

(b) In this same diagram, show what would happen to consumption expenditure if income increased to 200.

(c) Write the equation for the saving function and draw the saving function in a diagram.

(d) In this diagram show what would happen to savings if income increased from 200 to 250.

Exercise 6.2.   (a) Suppose the media predicts a deep and persistent economic recession. Households expect their future income and employment prospects to fall. They cut back on expenditure, reducing autonomous expenditure from 50 to 30. Re-draw the consumption and saving functions you have drawn in your diagrams for Exercise 6.1 to show the effects, if any, of this change in household behaviour.

(b) Suppose households also reduce the amount by which they are willing to spend out of any increase in income. In a diagram show the effect would this have on the consumption and savings functions you have drawn?

Exercise 6.3. The consumption function is $C = 50 + 0.75Y$ and investment is $I = 50$, exports are $X = 25$ and the import function is $IM = 20 + 0.25Y$.

(a) Write the equation for the aggregate expenditure function for this economy?

(b) Draw a diagram showing the aggregate expenditure function AE. What is the intercept of this function on the vertical axis?

(c) What is the slope of the AE function, and what does the slope measure?

Exercise 6.4. Output and income are in equilibrium when planned expenditures $C + I + X - IM$ are equal to national income, in other words, meaning $Y = $ AE.

(a) Suppose the consumption function is $C = 100 + 0.8Y$, investment is 25, exports are 30 and imports are $IM = 10 + 0.05Y$. Draw a diagram showing the aggregate expenditure function.

(b) In your diagram draw the 45° line that shows all points at which national income and aggregate expenditures are equal ($Y = $ AE).

(c) Using your diagram, or a numerical example, or an algebraic solution, find equilibrium output and income in this example and show it in the diagram.

Exercise 6.5. The diagram below shows the aggregate expenditure schedule for the economy and the equilibrium condition on the 45° line.

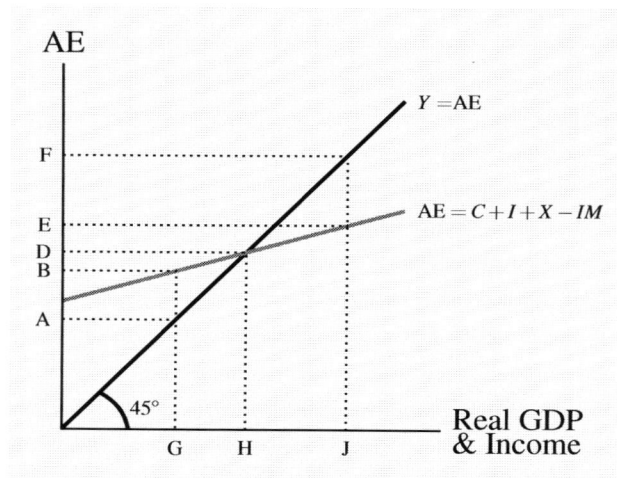

(a) Suppose output is 0G. What is the level of planned aggregate expenditure? Is planned expenditure greater or less than output?

(b) What is the size of the unplanned change in inventories at output 0G?

(c) How will business firms respond to this situation?

(d) What is the equilibrium income and expenditure?

(e) Suppose output is at 0J: What is there an unplanned change in inventories?

Exercise 6.6. The following diagram shows an economy that initially has an aggregate expenditure function AK.

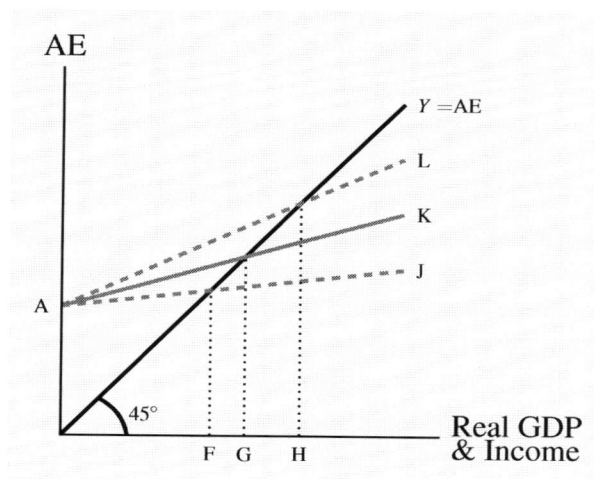

(a) What is the initial equilibrium real GDP?

(b) Suppose there is an increase in the marginal propensity to import. What is the new aggregate expenditure function?

(c) What is the new equilibrium real GDP and income?

(d) Suppose, instead, the marginal propensity to consume has increased. What is the new aggregate expenditure function? What is the new equilibrium real GDP and income?

Exercise 6.7. The distinction between autonomous and induced expenditure is important for the determination of equilibrium real GDP. Assume that the marginal propensity to consume is 0.80, the marginal propensity to import is 0.10 and autonomous aggregate expenditure is zero.

(a) What is the equation for the aggregate expenditure function under these assumptions?

(b) Draw the aggregate expenditure function in an income-expenditure 45° line diagram.

(c) What is the equilibrium level of real GDP illustrated by your diagram?

(d) Explain why this is the equilibrium level of real GDP.

Exercise 6.8. Suppose the marginal propensities to consume and import are 0.75 and 0.25. Starting from equilibrium, suppose planned investment increases by 10.

(a) By how much and in what direction does equilibrium income change?

(b) How much of that change in equilibrium income is the result of the change in consumption expenditure?

(c) How would your answers to (b) differ if the marginal propensity to consume were 0.85 rather than 0.75?

Exercise 6.9. Research by a team of expert economists has uncovered the consumption and import functions and produced a forecast of planned investment and exports for the economy of Wonderland as reported below.

Real GDP	Consumption	Investment	Exports	Imports
Y	C	I	X	IM
0	100	100	75	25
800	920	100	75	145
900	1010	100	75	160
1000	1100	100	75	175
1100	1190	100	75	190
1200	1280	100	75	205

(a) What equilibrium real GDP would Wonderland produce?

(b) What are the marginal propensities to consume and import in Wonderland?

(c) What is the size of the multiplier?

(d) If actual GDP were 900, what difference between planned and actual investment would result? Why?

(e) If planned investment increased by 50 to 100, what would happen to equilibrium income?

Exercise 6.10. Planned investment is 100, exports are 50 and saving is $S = -25 + 0.2Y$ and imports are $IM = 25 + 0.3Y$.

(a) Draw a diagram showing the initial equilibrium level of income.

(b) Now households decide to increase their saving at every level of income, but do not change their marginal propensity to save. Using the diagram show what happens to equilibrium income and to household saving?

Exercise 6.11. Suppose there is no autonomous expenditure in the economy. The aggregate expenditure function is $AE = 0.75Y$.

(a) Draw the aggregate expenditure function and the 45° line in a diagram.

(b) What is the equilibrium level of real output and income?

(c) How would you explain your answer to part b).

EXERCISES FOR CHAPTER 7

Exercise 7.1. Suppose a government is established in a country where none previously existed. The government spends 100, financed by borrowing, to provide public services. If autonomous consumption, investment and exports minus imports are 200 and the marginal propensity to consume $MPC = 0.75$, and the $MPM = 0.15$, what are the equilibrium real GDP values before and after the government is established.

Exercise 7.2. If the government expenditure in Exercise 7.1 were financed by imposing a net tax rate on income of $t = 0.10$:

   (a) Calculate and compare the slopes of the AE functions in Exercises 7.1 and 7.2.

   (b) Calculate and compare the multipliers in Exercises 7.1 and 7.2.

   (c) What is the equilibrium real GDP in Exercise 7.2 compared to Exercise 7.1.

Exercise 7.3. If government expenditure is 100 and the net tax rate is $t = 0.20$:

   (a) Complete the following table:

Y	$NT = tY$	G	$BB = NT - G$
100			
200			
300			
400			
500			
600			
700			

   (b) In a diagram with national income Y on the horizontal axis and government revenue and expenditure on the vertical axis, draw the government expenditure and net tax functions. Explain the intercept on the vertical axis, and the slope you have given to the NT and G functions in your diagram.

   (c) Suppose the government cuts the tax rate to $t = 0.15$. Show the effects in your diagram.

Exercise 7.4. Draw diagrams to illustrate the initial equilibrium national income, the effect of the increase in government expenditure on equilibrium national income, and the government's budget functions and balances before and after the increase in government expenditure.

Exercise 7.5. Suppose the government raises its revenue by a net tax of 25 percent on income, $t = 0.25$, the marginal propensity to consume out of disposable income is 0.8 and the marginal propensity to import is $m = 0.15$.

(a) What is the slope of the AE function? What is the size of the multiplier?

(b) Autonomous expenditure by the non-government sectors $(C_0 + I_0 + X_0 - IM_0)$ is 300 and government expenditure is 400. What is the equilibrium income and output? What is the government's budget balance?

(c) The government increases its expenditures by 100 to provide additional funding for national defense. What is the effect on equilibrium income and output? What is the effect on the government's budget balance?

Exercise 7.6. An economy is in equilibrium at a real GDP of 750, but current estimates put potential output at $Y_P = 850$.

(a) Is there an inflationary or a recessionary gap, and, if there is either, what is its size?

(b) Research suggests that the MPC is 0.75, the MPM is 0.10, and the net tax rate is 0.20. If there is a gap, what change in government expenditure would eliminate the gap?

(c) If the government preferred to change its net tax rate to eliminate the gap, and not change government expenditure, what new tax rate would be required to eliminate the gap?

Exercise 7.7. (a) Draw a diagram that shows the government's budget balance relative to national income. Explain briefly the vertical intercept of the budget function and its slope.

(b) Using your diagram from (b), show the structural budget balance and a situation in which the actual balance is different from the structural balance.

(c) Based on this diagram, show and explain the difference between the budget effects of automatic stabilization and discretionary fiscal policy.

Exercise 7.8. Suppose the $MPC = 0.8$, the tax rate $t = 0.1$, the $MPM = 0.12$ and autonomous aggregate expenditure $A = 1000$, including government expenditure $G = 20$. Further assume the government has an outstanding public debt of 1000.

(a) What is the initial debt to GDP or debt to national income ratio?

(b) Suppose government increased its expenditure by $\Delta G = 10$, without any increase in the tax rate. What are the new equilibrium national income and the government's new budget balance?

(c) What is the outstanding public debt and the public debt ratio at the new equilibrium income, assuming the economy has reached its new equilibrium national income in one year?

EXERCISES FOR CHAPTER 8

Exercise 8.1. What are the functions of money? What is money in Canada today? What is the money supply in Canada today? Are debit cards and credit cards money?

Exercise 8.2. Since both central banks and commercial banks can create money what is the key difference between a central bank, like the Bank of Canada, and the many commercial banks in the financial industry?

Exercise 8.3. Suppose the banks receive $100 cash from a new deposit of funds previously held outside the banking system. If banks operate with a 5 percent reserve ratio, use simple balance sheets to show by how much this new cash would affect lending and deposits of all banks in the system.

Exercise 8.4. If banks have a 10 percent reserve ratio and the public has a 10 percent currency ratio how much lending and deposit creation can the undertake after they receive a new $1,000 cash deposit. How much would the public's holding of cash increase? Would it be in the banks' interest to find ways to reduce the currency ratio? Why?

Exercise 8.5. What protection does the Canadian Deposit Insurance Corporation provide for your money if your bank is unable to pay cash to its depositors?

Exercise 8.6. Define the money multiplier and explain how it might be used.

Exercise 8.7. Suppose the banks in the banking system find it prudent to maintain holdings of cash equal to 10 percent of their deposit liabilities, and people find it convenient to hold cash balances equal to 15 percent.

   (a) If the monetary base in the economy is $1,000, what is the size of the money supply?

   (b) Suppose the monetary base decreased by $100, would the money supply change? If so, by how much would it change?

Exercise 8.8. Suppose a crisis in financial markets, like the collapse of the asset back commercial paper (ABCP) market in 2007 and 2008, increases the risk banks attach to lending and the non-bank public attaches to bank deposits. What are the implications for the desired reserve ratio, the currency ratio and the money supply multiplier and the money supply?

Exercise 8.9. Using a diagram illustrate and explain the determinants of the position and slope of the money supply function assuming an initial monetary base of $1000, $rr = 5\%$ and $cr = 10\%$. If the monetary base were to increase by 10% how would the money supply and the money supply function in your diagram change?

Exercise 8.10. Suppose the currency ratio depends on the interest rate such that the non-bank public reduces their cash holdings relative to deposits (cr) as the interest rate rises. Use a diagram to illustrate what effect if any this condition would have on the money supply function.

EXERCISES FOR CHAPTER 9

Exercise 9.1. If the current market interest rate is 3 percent and a bond promises a coupon of $3 each year in perpetuity (forever), what is the current market price of the bond?

Exercise 9.2. Suppose you are holding a bond that will pay $5 each year for the next two years from today and mature two years from today.

    (a) If current two-year market interest rates are 4 percent, what is the market price of your bond?

    (b) If market interest rates rise tomorrow to 6 percent, what will be the market price of your bond?

    (c) What is the "market risk" in holding bonds?

Exercise 9.3. You are holding a cash balance that you want to place in the bond market for a period of three years. The market rate of interest on three year bonds today is 5.5 percent. Would you be willing to pay $1,015 for a $1,000 bond with a 6 percent coupon maturing three years from today? Explain your answer.

Exercise 9.4. Draw a diagram to illustrate the relationship between the demand for real money balances and the interest rate, $L = kY - hi$ when real GDP has a given value Y_0.

    (a) Explain your choice of the intersection of your demand for money function with the horizontal axis, and your choice of the slope of the function.

    (b) Using your diagram, illustrate and explain the quantity of real money balances demanded for a specific interest rate, say i_0. Pay particular attention to the underlying motives for holding these money balances.

    (c) Suppose interest rates declined from your initial assumption of i_0 to a new lower rate i_1. Illustrate and explain the effect of the change in interest rates on the demand for money balances.

    (d) Holding interest rates constant at either i_0 or i_1, suppose real GDP were to increase. Illustrate and explain the effect of the increase in real GDP on the demand function and the quantity of real money balances people hold.

Exercise 9.5. Draw a diagram to illustrate equilibrium in the money market.

    (a) Starting from your initial equilibrium, suppose real national income increased. Illustrate and explain how the money market would adjust to this change in economic conditions.

    (b) How does the interest rate in the new equilibrium compare with the interest rate in the initial equilibrium?

Exercise 9.6. Draw a diagram to illustrate the foreign exchange market in which Euros are bought with or sold for Canadian dollars, assuming the current exchange rate is $1.54Cdn=1 Euro. Starting from that equilibrium exchange rate, suppose Canadian interest rates fall relative to European rates. Using your foreign exchange market, show how the dollar-euro exchange rates would be affected.

Exercise 9.7. Construct a set of diagrams that shows the monetary transmission mechanism linking interest rates to aggregate demand and output. Using these diagrams, show and explain:

(a) How a reduction in the money supply would affect aggregate demand and output.

(b) Alternatively, how an increase in the precautionary demand for money balances caused by terrorist activity, or severe weather events, or an increase in uncertainty in general would affect aggregate demand and output. Assume the money supply is held constant.

(c) Alternatively, how an increase in autonomous investment expenditure and exports would affect interest rates, aggregate demand, and output.

EXERCISES FOR CHAPTER 10

Exercise 10.1. Explain carefully why a central bank does not operate to make a profit but a commercial bank does. What is the central bank's operating objective? What unique power does a central bank have that allows it to pursue its operating objective?

Exercise 10.2. Explain carefully why a central bank's power to conduct monetary policy is based on its unique position as supplier of the monetary base.

Exercise 10.3. Why would a change in the monetary base ΔMB cause a change in the money supply?

Exercise 10.4. (a) Suppose a central bank buys $10 million on the open market. What effect does this have on the monetary base and the reserve position of the commercial banks?

  (b) If the banks hold reserves equal to 2.5 percent of their deposit liabilities, and the public holds cash equal to 7.5 percent of their deposit holdings, calculate the effect of this open-market transaction on:

    (a) The money supply

    (b) The public's cash balances

    (c) The banks' reserve balances

Exercise 10.5. Suppose the central bank decides to use its power to set interest rates. Use a money market diagram to show and explain what happens to the real money supply if real output increases $(\Delta Y > 0)$ and the central bank maintains a constant interest rate.

Exercise 10.6. (a) What is the Bank of Canada's monetary policy target?

  (b) What monetary policy instrument does the Bank use to pursue this target?

  (c) What do the Bank's procedures for implementing policy mean for its control over money supply?

Exercise 10.7. Use a diagram to show circumstances in the market for overnight funds that might lead the Bank of Canada to make an SRA. Why would the Bank use an SRA in this case rather than an open market operation?

Exercise 10.8. Suppose a central bank decides to conduct monetary policy according to a Taylor rule for interest rates.

  (a) How does it choose the basic setting for the interest rate within the rule?

  (b) How would it respond to a rise in the unemployment rate?

  (c) How would the bank react to an inflation rate higher than its target inflation rate?

  (d) Why would the bank decide to change the basic setting of its interest rate?

Exercise 10.9. Use diagrams to show and explain how monetary policy conducted according to a Taylor rule would stabilize real output at potential output.

EXERCISES FOR CHAPTER 11

Exercise 11.1. Assume the central bank conducts monetary policy by setting a nominal money supply.

(a) Use a money-market diagram to show how changes in the general price level (P) would affect the equilibrium interest rate.

(b) Use a 45° line diagram to show how changes in expenditure caused by the changes in interest rates in (a) would change equilibrium real GDP.

(c) Combining the results from parts a) and b), construct an AD curve that shows combinations of real GDP and the general price level when autonomous expenditures and money supply are constant.

Exercise 11.2. Draw diagrams for a demand for money and an interest rate/expenditure function that show conditions under which changes in the general price level cause large changes in aggregate expenditure and equilibrium real GDP.

Exercise 11.3. Do you agree that a flatter AE curve (a lower value for the slope) would result in a steeper AD curve? Explain why.

Exercise 11.4. Consider a numerical example of an AD curve when the central bank sets the money supply: $AE = 100 + 0.5Y + 0.2(M/P)$, and $M = 500$.

(a) Suppose the nominal money supply $M = 500$. Find and write the AE function for each of the price levels 1.0, 2.0, and 3.0.

(b) Explain why a change in the price level changes planned aggregate expenditure.

(c) Based on the equilibrium condition $Y = AE$, plot combinations of P and Y in a diagram and draw the AD curve.

(d) Suppose an increase in investment increased autonomous expenditure by 25. Plot the new AD curve in your diagram.

Exercise 11.5. Consider a numerical example of a short run aggregate supply curve (AS) for an economy in which producers are price setters as follows: $P = 100 + 1.5 \times W/(Y/N)$. Assume the money wage rate $W = \$1000$, and labour productivity (Y/N) declines as employment and output increases according to: $Y/N = 200 - 10N$. This gives the following values: $Y = 360, Y/N = 180$; $Y = 640, Y/N = 160$; $Y = 840, Y/N = 140$.

(a) Calculate the price level P for each income level given, and plot the resulting AS curve in a diagram.

(b) Explain the reason for the change in the price level as real output Y increases and the economy moves along the AS curve.

(c) Suppose the money wage rate increased by 10 percent from $1000 to $1100. Calculate the price levels for incomes of $Y = 360$, 640 and 840 and plot this AS curve in the same diagram used in part a).

(d) What effect does a change in money wage rates have on the AS curve? Why?

Exercise 11.6. An economy has the following aggregate demand and short-run aggregate supply conditions: AD: $Y = 1000 - 30P$, and AS: $Y = 500P - 6950$

(a) Plot the AD and AS functions in a diagram.

(b) What are the equilibrium values for real GDP and the price level?

(c) If potential output is $Y_P = 650$, what type of output gap, if any, do you observe?

(d) Suppose research reveals that the aggregate expenditure function underlying the AD curve has a slope $[c(1-t) - m] = 0.5$. What change, if any, in the expenditure component of fiscal policy would be needed to eliminate any observed output gap?

Exercise 11.7. Use an AD/AS diagram for an economy in short run equilibrium at potential output Y_P, to illustrate and explain the effect of a fall in international demand for the economy's manufactured exports. What type of output gap, if any, is caused by the fall in exports?

Exercise 11.8. Explain why a fall in the money wage rate might not reduce or eliminate a recessionary gap and might in fact make the gap larger.

Exercise 11.9. Explain why a rise in the money wage rate might work to eliminate an inflationary gap.

Exercise 11.10. Use diagrams to show a monetary policy that manages the money base using a McCallum rule $MB = MB_0 - \mu(Y - Y_P)$ and the corresponding AD curve in an AD/AS/Y_P model.

Exercise 11.11. Use diagrams to show how the central bank following a McCallum rule would change monetary policy to reduce or eliminate an inflationary gap.

Exercise 11.12. Use a government budget function to show how an output gap affects the government's budget balance.

Exercise 11.13. Using a diagram, illustrate the difference, if any, between the actual budget balance and the structural budget balance for an economy with an inflationary gap.

Exercise 11.14. If the Finance Minister's changes fiscal policy to remove a recessionary gap, use a diagram to show the new budget function and the actual and structural balances that result.

EXERCISES FOR CHAPTER 12

Exercise 12.1. Use a diagram to illustrate the equilibrium inflation rate. In this diagram, show how a permanent increase in export demand would affect the equilibrium inflation rate, if the central bank did not react and change its monetary policy. If the central bank did react to this change in the equilibrium inflation rate to defend its inflation target, what change in the interest rate setting and money supply growth would you observe? How would this change in the interest rate setting affect ADπ and the composition of ADπ?

Exercise 12.2. If careful research estimates potential output Y_P at 1000, and the ADπ function is $Y = 1,150 - 25\pi$, what is the equilibrium inflation rate? If the central bank's inflation rate target is 4.0 what change in the interest rate must the central bank make to defend its inflation target?

Exercise 12.3. Suppose opportunities for investing in high tech applications boost aggregate demand in the short run, and aggregate supply in the long run. Using ASπ and ADπ curves with equilibrium at potential output, show why output might rise without much of an increase in inflation.

Exercise 12.4. Suppose a new round of labour negotiations results in a higher average rate of increase in money wage rates for the next three years. Illustrate and explain how this would affect short-run aggregate supply conditions and the ASπ curve.

Exercise 12.5. Draw an aggregate supply and demand curve diagram to show an economy in short run equilibrium at potential output. Suppose a wide-spread recession reduces incomes in foreign countries, leading to reduced demand for exports. Illustrate and explain how this would affect the short run equilibrium Y and π in your diagram.

Exercise 12.6. Suppose central banks have reduced their policy interest rates to the lower bound to fight a deep and prolonged recession. Use a diagram to show how either a reduction in the inflation rate, or deflation, would change the slope of the ADπ curve. Would cuts in nominal money wage rates and further reductions in the inflation rate reduce the recessionary gap when the central bank is constrained by the lower bound on its interest rate?

Exercise 12.7. In the two years before 2008 the federal government reduced the GST from 7 percent to 5 percent. Use an ADπ/ASπ/Y_P diagram to illustrate and explain the effects of this tax change on equilibrium output and inflation. If the economy was in equilibrium at Y_P and the target inflation rate π^* before the tax cut, what monetary policy action, if any, would the central bank make to maintain those equilibrium conditions after the tax cut? What short run net benefit, it any, would households and businesses realize as a result of the cut in the GST?

Exercise 12.8. Suppose the federal government wants to stabilize the public debt ratio at its current level. The change in the public debt ratio (Δpd) is given by: $\Delta pd = -spbb + (i - n)pd$, where $spbb$ is the structural primary budget balance, i is the interest rate on outstanding government bonds and n is the annual rate of growth of Y.

    (a) What is the $spbb$ required to make $\Delta pd = 0$?

(b) Suppose the rate of growth of Y falls. What change in fiscal policy as measured by the *spbb* is required to maintain the public debt ratio?

(c) How would this policy change affect $AD\pi$?

(d) What support might monetary policy give to the government's $\Delta pd = 0$ policy?

EXERCISES FOR CHAPTER 13

Exercise 13.1. (a) What is the distinction between growth in potential GDP and growth in per capita real GDP?

(b) Why is this distinction important to an evaluation of the relationship between economic growth and growth in standards of living?

(c) Which grows more rapidly, potential GDP or per capita real GDP?

Exercise 13.2. Consider two countries with the same level of potential GDP, say $100 billion, today. Suppose potential GDP grows at an annual rate of 3.5 percent (0.0325) in one country and 3.25 percent (0.035) in the second country. Based on this information:

(a) What do you predict for the percentage difference in potential GDP between the two countries 10 years in the future?

(b) 20 years in the future? [Note that the growth rates will compound to determine real GDP according to the following formula: $Y_t = Y_0(1 + \text{growth rate})^t$.]

Exercise 13.3. Suppose you have the following information about an economy:

Average annual rates of growth from 1998 to 2008:

Potential GDP	3.5%
Labour force	2.1%
Capital stock	3.0%

Share of labour income in national income: 2/3. Using growth accounting, find the contribution to the annual growth in potential GDP that came from:

(a) Growth in labour force

(b) Growth in capital stock

(c) Improved productivity as measured by the Solow residual.

Exercise 13.4. If technology were constant while labour force grew at a rate of 2.5% a year, capital stock grew at 1.5% per year and the share of labour income in national income was 70%, how fast would potential GDP grow?

Exercise 13.5. Suppose you have the following information for two economies:

		Country A	Country B
Average annual	i. Labour force	2.5%	4.0%
growth rates:	ii. Capital stock	3.5%	3.5%
Labour income/national income:		2/3	2/3

(a) Assuming a constant state of technology, which of these two countries will have the faster rate of growth in total real GDP?

(b) Which of the two countries will have the faster rate of growth in per capita real GDP?

(c) What differences, if any, do you see in the growth rates of the capital to labour ratios in the two countries?

(d) Explain the reasons for the differences in growth rates you have found?

Exercise 13.6. In Wonderland labour force and capital stock both grow at the rate of 2.5% a year but technology is constant. At what rate will potential GDP grow? At what rate will per capita GDP grow? If improvements in technology increased total factor productivity by 1.5% year, how fast would per capita real GDP grow?

Exercise 13.7.   (a) Why do economists emphasize that improvements in technology are the key to improvements in standards of living?

(b) Using a diagram that shows the relationship between capital per worker and output per worker, illustrate and explain why growth in capital per worker cannot provide sustained growth in output per worker and standards of living.

(c) In the diagram in (b), show how an improvement in productivity coming from improved technology could provide sustained increases in standards of living.

Exercise 13.8. Suppose an economy has the following conditions:

Per worker GDP: $y = k^{1/3}$
Savings per worker: $s = 0.2y$
Population and labour force growth: $n = 0.05$

(a) What is the steady-state level of output per worker, y?

(b) What is the rate of growth of total GDP required for the steady state?

(c) If savings increased to $s_1 = 0.25y$, what new steady-state output would result?

(d) What is the rate of growth of total GDP required for the new steady state?

(e) Use a diagram to show the steady-state output per worker in (a) and in (c).

Exercise 13.9. (a) Explain the convergence hypothesis.

(b) Why does the convergence hypothesis anticipate faster growth in standards of living in the lower per capita income OECD countries than in the higher per capita income OECD countries?

(c) Does the convergence hypothesis offer hope for improved standards of living in poor African countries? Why or why not?

EXERCISES FOR CHAPTER 14

Exercise 14.1. Suppose a country has a current account surplus of $20 billion, but a capital account deficit of $18 billion.

(a) Is its balance of payments in deficit or surplus? Why?

(b) What change in official exchange reserves would you see? Why?

(c) Is the central bank buying or selling foreign currency?

(d) What effect does the central bank's foreign currency purchase or sale have on the monetary base? Explain why?

Exercise 14.2. Assume the initial exchange rate is $1.20CDN for $1.00U.S. After 10 years, the United States price level has risen from 100 to 200, and the Canadian price level has risen from 100 to 175. What was the inflation rate in each country? What nominal exchange rate would preserve the initial real exchange rate? Which country's currency depreciated?

Exercise 14.3. Suppose portfolio managers shift $100 million in assets under their control out of Canadian government securities and into United States government securities. What change would this portfolio shift make in the Canadian balance of payments?

Exercise 14.4. What is the expected rate of appreciation of the US dollar if interest rate parity prevails and Canadian nominal interest rates are 1 percent higher than United States interest rates?

Exercise 14.5. Explain the "interest parity condition." If Canadian interest rates are 1.5 percentage points lower than United States interest rates, what change in the international value of the Canadian dollar would you predict?

Exercise 14.6. Suppose natural gas and crude oil prices were to drop sharply and expectations were they would remain low. Use a foreign exchange market diagram to show the effect on the Canadian/US dollar exchange rate?

Exercise 14.7. Using a diagram to illustrate:

(a) The demand for foreign exchange and the demand curve for foreign exchange.

(b) The supply of foreign exchange and the supply curve for foreign exchange.

(c) The equilibrium exchange rate.

Exercise 14.8. Use a foreign exchange market diagram to show equilibrium with a flexible or floating exchange rate to show:

(a) How a decline in exports would affect the foreign exchange rate?

(b) How exports and imports would change to give balance of payments equilibrium at the new equilibrium exchange rate?

(c) The effects, if any, on the holdings of official reserves.

Exercise 14.9. Use a foreign exchange market diagram to show:

(a) Equilibrium with a fixed exchange rate.

(b) The effect of a decline in exports on conditions in the foreign exchange market when the exchange rate is fixed.

(c) The amount of the purchase or sale of foreign exchange reserves required if the central bank defends the fixed exchange rate.

(d) The effects change in the holdings of official reserves and the monetary base as a result of the defence of the fixed exchange rate.

Exercise 14.10. Use AD/AS and foreign exchange market diagrams to show why monetary policy is powerful and fiscal policy is weak when a country has a flexible exchange rate regime.

Exercise 14.11. Use AD/AS and foreign exchange market diagrams to show why the choice of a fixed exchange rate makes fiscal policy a more powerful tool for demand management. What happens to the domestic money supply when a government austerity program cuts its expenditures on goods and services and raises taxes?

EXERCISES FOR CHAPTER 15

Exercise 15.1. The following table shows the labour input requirements to produce a bushel of wheat and a litre of wine in two countries, Northland and Southland, on the assumption of constant cost production technology – meaning that the production possibility curves in each are straight lines.

Labour requirements per unit produced		
	Northland	Southland
Per bushel of wheat	1	3
Per litre of wine	2	4

(a) Which country has an absolute advantage in the production of both wheat and wine?

(b) What is the opportunity cost of wheat in each economy? Of wine?

(c) What is the pattern of comparative advantage here?

(d) Suppose the country with a comparative advantage in wine reduces wheat production by one bushel and reallocates the labour involved to wine production. How much additional wine does it produce?

(e) Which country, if either, gains from this change in production and trade, and what is the gain?

(f) If the country with the comparative advantage in wheat reduced wine production enough to increase wheat production by one bushel, how much wine could it get by selling the additional bushel of wheat to the other country at that economy's opportunity cost?

Exercise 15.2. Canada and the United States can produce two goods, xylophones and yogourt. Each good can be produced with labour alone. Canada requires 60 hours to produce a ton of yogourt and 6 hours to produce a xylophone. The United States requires 40 hours to produce the ton of yogourt and 5 hours to produce a xylophone.

(a) Describe the state of absolute advantage between these economies in producing goods.

(b) In which good does Canada have a comparative advantage? Does this mean the United States has a comparative advantage in the other good?

(c) Draw the production possibility frontier for each economy to scale on a diagram, assuming that each economy has an endowment of 240 hours of labour.

(d) On the same diagram, draw Canada's consumption possibility frontier on the assumption that it can trade with the United States at the United States rate of transformation.

(e) Draw the US consumption possibility frontier under the assumption that it can trade at Canada's rate of transformation.

Exercise 15.3. The domestic demand for bicycles is given by $P = 36 - 0.3Q$. The foreign supply is given by $P = 18$ and domestic supply by $P = 16 + 0.4Q$.

(a) Illustrate the market equilibrium on a diagram, and compute the amounts supplied by domestic and foreign suppliers.

(b) If the government now imposes a tariff of $6 per unit on the foreign good, illustrate the impact geometrically, and compute the new quantities supplied by domestic and foreign producers.

(c) In the diagram, illustrate the area representing tariff revenue and compute its value.

Exercise 15.4. In Exercise 15.3, illustrate the deadweight losses associated with the imposition of the tariff, and compute the amounts.

(a) Compute the additional amount of profit made by the domestic producer as a result of the tariff. [Hint: refer to Figure 15.4 in the text.]

Exercise 15.5. The domestic demand for office printers is given by $P = 40 - 0.2Q$. The supply of domestic producers is given by $P = 12 + 0.1Q$, and international supply by $P = 20$.

(a) Illustrate this market geometrically.

(b) Compute total demand and the amounts supplied by domestic and foreign suppliers.

(c) If the government gives a production subsidy of $2 per unit to domestic suppliers in order to increase their competitiveness, calculate the new amounts supplied by domestic and foreign producers. [Hint: The domestic supply curve becomes $P = 10 + 0.1Q$].

(d) Compute the cost to the government of this scheme.

Exercise 15.6. The domestic demand for turnips is given by $P = 128 - (1/2)Q$. The market supply of domestic suppliers is given by $P = 12 + (1/4)Q$, and the world price is $32 per bushel.

(a) First graph this market and then solve for the equilibrium quantity purchased.

(b) How much of the quantity traded will be produced domestically and how much will be imported?

(c) Assume now that a quota of 76 units is put in place. Illustrate the resulting market equilibrium graphically.

(d) Compute the domestic price of turnips and the associated quantity traded with the quota in place. [Hint: you could shrink the demand curve in towards the origin by the amount of the quota and equate the result with the domestic supply curve].

Exercise 15.7. The domestic market for cheese is given by $P = 108 - 2Q$ and $P = 16 + 1/4Q$. These are the demand and supply conditions. The good can be supplied internationally at a constant price $P = 20$.

(a) Illustrate the domestic market in the absence of trade and solve for the equilibrium price and quantity.

(b) With free trade illustrate the market graphically and compute the total amount purchased, and the amounts supplied by domestic and international suppliers.

(c) Suppose now that the government implements a price floor in the domestic market equal to $28. Illustrate the market outcome graphically.

(d) For the outcome with a price floor, compute the quantity supplied by domestic and international suppliers respectively.

Exercise 15.8. The following are hypothetical production possibilities tables for Canada and the United States. For each line required, plot any two or more points on the line.

	Canada					United States			
	A	B	C	D		A	B	C	D
Peaches	0	5	10	15	**Peaches**	0	10	20	30
Apples	30	20	10	0	**Apples**	15	10	5	0

(a) Plot Canada's production possibilities curve by plotting at least 2 points on the curve.

(b) Plot the United States' production possibilities curve by plotting at least 2 points on the curve on the graph above.

(c) What is each country's cost ratio of producing Peaches and Apples?

(d) Which economy should specialize in which product?

(e) Plot the United States' trading possibilities curve (by plotting at least 2 points on the curve) if the actual terms of the trade are 1 apple for 1 peach.

(f) Plot the Canada' trading possibilities curve (by plotting at least 2 points on the curve) if the actual terms of the trade are 1 apple for 1 peach.

(g) Suppose that the optimum product mixes before specialization and trade were B in the United States and C in Canada. What are the gains from specialization and trade?

Solutions to exercises for Chapter 1

Exercise 1.1.

(a) If all 100 workers make cakes their output is $100 \times 4 = 400$.

(b) If all workers make shirts their output is $100 \times 3 = 300$.

(c) The diagram shows the *PPF* for this economy.

(d) As illustrated in the diagram.

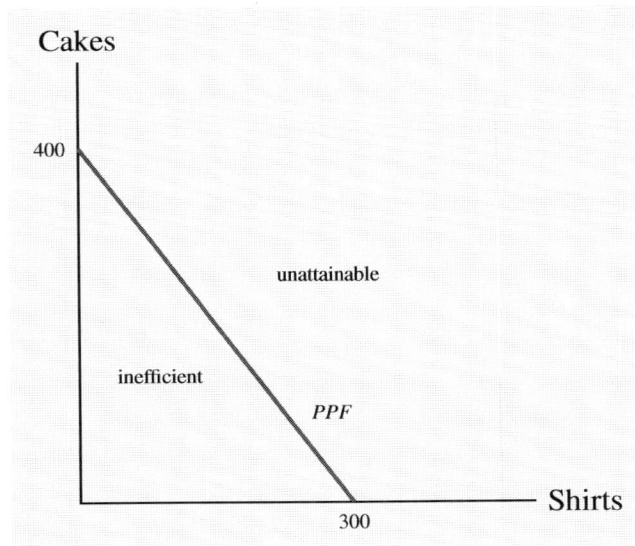

Exercise 1.2.

(a) The *PPF* is curved outwards with intercepts of 1000 on the Thinkpod axis and 6000 on the iPad axis. Each point on the *PPF* shows one combination of outputs.

(b) Different.

(c) 400 X.

(d) The new *PPF* in the diagram has the same Thinkpod intercept, 1000, but a new iPad intercept of 7200.

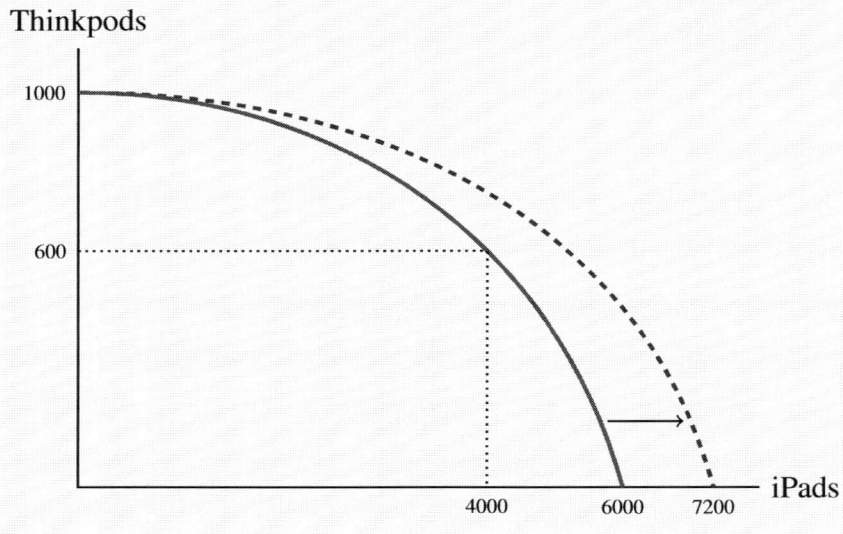

Exercise 1.3. By examining the opportunity cost in the region where the combinations are defined, and by assuming a linear trade-off between each set of combinations, it can be seen that the first combination in the table is feasible, but not the second combination.

Exercise 1.4.

(a) $50.

(b) $60.

(c) See diagram.

(d) See diagram.

(e) The person with the lower wage.

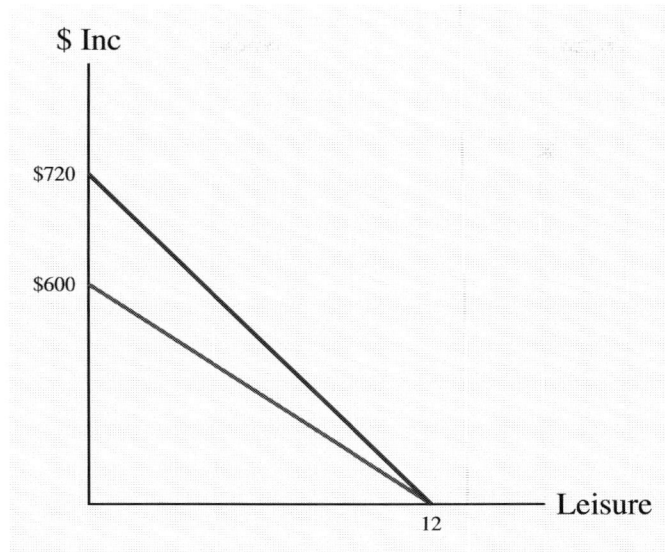

Exercise 1.5.

(a) Louis has an advantage in cutting the grass while Carrie Anne should wash cars.

(b) If they each work a twelve-hour day, between them they can cut 12 lawns and wash 24 cars.

Exercise 1.6. Following the method described in the text:

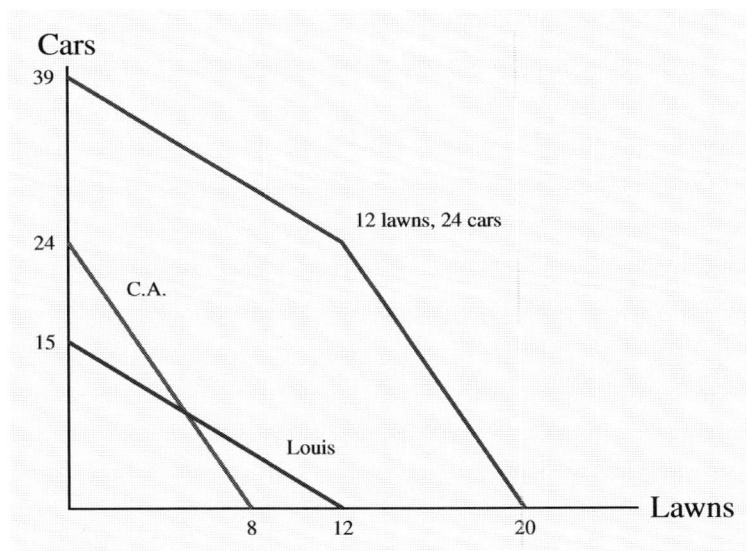

Exercise 1.7.

(a) Carrie Anne's lawn intercept is now 12 rather than 8.

(b) Yes, specialization still matters because C.A. is more efficient at cars.

(c) The new coordinates will be 39 on the vertical axis, 24 on the horizontal axis and the kink point is the same.

Exercise 1.8. C.A.'s intercepts are now 30 cars and 15 lawns; Louis' intercepts are 18.75 cars and 15 lawns; the economy-wide *PPF* car coordinate is thus 48.75, the lawn coordinate is 30, and the kink point is 15 lawns and 30 cars.

Exercise 1.9.

(a) 220 cakes requires 55 workers, the remaining 45 workers can produce 135 shirts. Hence this combination lies inside the *PPF* described in Exercise 1.1.

(b) 98 workers.

(c) 2%.

Solutions to exercises for Chapter 2

Exercise 2.1. These variables are positively related.

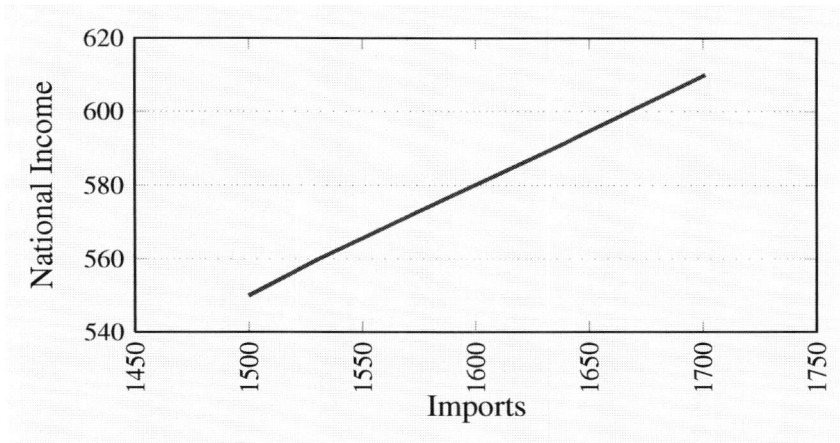

Exercise 2.2. For (b) the answer is 32%, and for (c) the answer is 5.26%.

Year	2005	2006	2007	2008	2009	2010	2011	2012	2013	2014
Index	0.95	1.00	1.04	1.09	1.14	1.14	1.21	1.23	1.32	1.35

Exercise 2.3. To find the national unemployment rate for each year you take a weighted average of the unemployment rate in the big cities and that in other areas. The weights used are the shares of population living in each area. In 2007, for example, the national unemployment rate would be: Big city rate $\times 0.67 +$ other rate $\times 0.33 = 5 \times 0.67 + 7 \times 0.33 = 5.67$. Hence:

Year	2007	2008	2009	2010	2011
Index	5.67	7.99	8.33	10.67	9.67

Exercise 2.4. For years 1 through 5 the index values for transport, rent and food are:

	Yr 1	Yr 2	Yr 3	Yr 4	Yr 5	Weight in total expenditure
Transport	100	100	107	107	107	10%
Rent	100	100	110	112	115	55%
Food	100	103	102	107	110	35%

The aggregate price index is the weighted average of the component price indexes with weights equal to shares in total expenditure. For Year 1 the aggregate index is $(100 \times 0.10 + 100 \times 0.55 + 100 \times 0.35) = 100$. For years 2 through 5 this methodology gives aggregate price indexes of 101, 108, 110, 114.

Exercise 2.5.

	2000	2002	2004	2006	2008	2010
Nominal	100	111.54	126.92	126.92	119.23	115.38
Carrot price $	2.6	2.9	3.3	3.3	3.1	3
CPI	110	112	115	117	120	124
CPI new base	100	101.82	104.55	106.36	109.09	112.73
Real carrot index	100	109.55	121.40	119.33	109.29	102.36

Exercise 2.6. The scatter diagram plots observed combinations of income and consumption as follows. For parts (c) and (d): the variables are positively related and the causation runs from income to consumption.

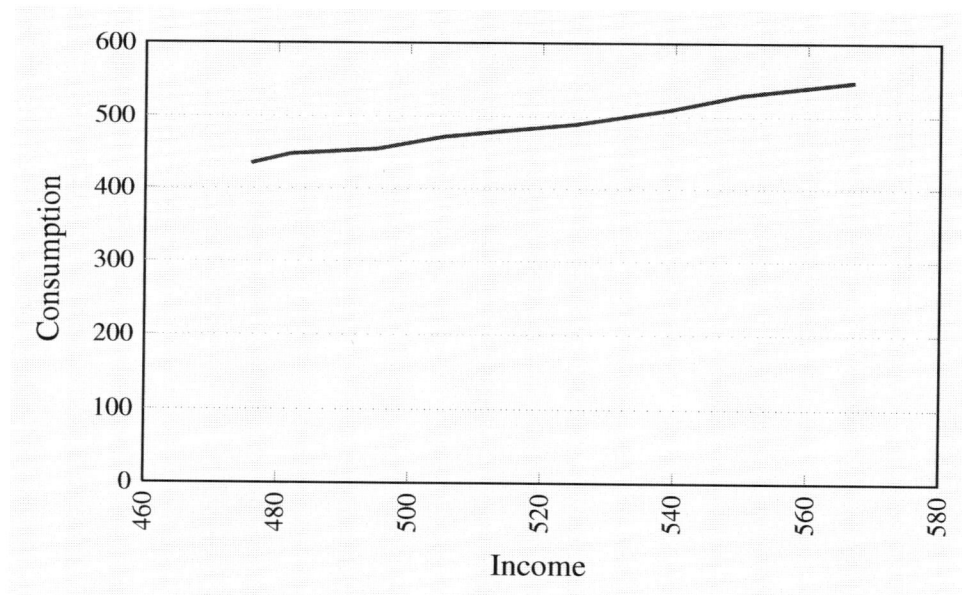

Exercise 2.7. The percentage changes in income are:

| Pct Inc | 1.3 | 2.7 | 2.0 | 4.0 | 2.7 | 2.0 | 3.1 |
| Pct Con | 3.0 | 1.6 | 3.7 | 3.8 | 4.1 | 4.1 | 3.4 |

Exercise 2.8. The relationship given by the equation $Y = 10 + 2X$ when plotted has an intercept on the vertical (Y) axis of 10 and the slope of the line is 2. The maximum value of Y (where X is 12) is 34.

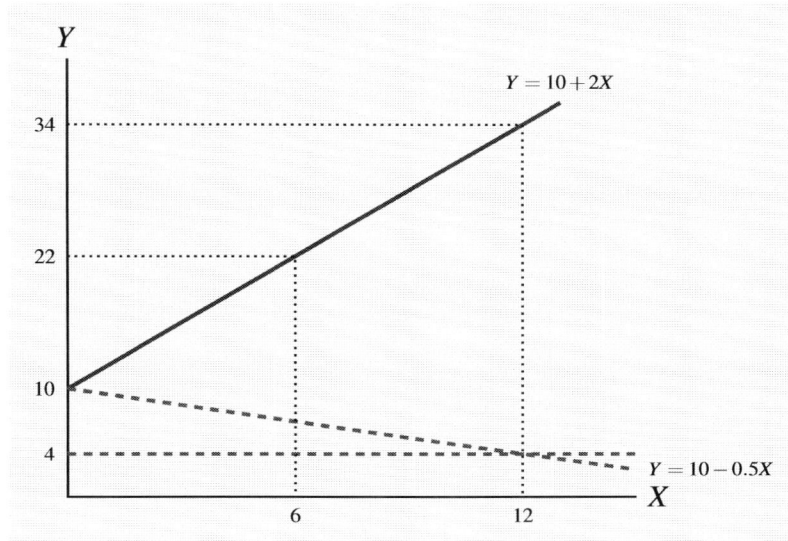

X	0	1	2	3	4	5	6	7	8	9	10	11	12
Y	10	12	14	16	18	20	22	24	26	28	30	32	34

Exercise 2.9. The relationship $Y = 10 - 0.5X$ has a Y intercept of 10 but there is now a negative slope equal to one half (-0.5). When X has a value of 12, Y has a value of 4. If you plot this in the diagram for Exercise 2.8 it is the dashed line sloping downward from 10 to 4 at $X = 12$.

Exercise 2.10.

(a) The relationship is negative.

(b) The relationship is non-linear.

Solutions to exercises for Chapter 3

Exercise 3.1.

(a) The diagram shows the supply and demand curves from the data in the table. These curves intersect at the equilibrium price \$32 and the equilibrium quantity 7.

(b) Excess demand is 6 and excess supply is 3.

(c) With excess demand the price is bid up, with excess supply the price is pushed down.

(d) Equate supply P to demand: $18 + 2Q = 60 - 4Q$, implying $6Q = 42$, which is $Q = 7$. Hence $P = 32$.

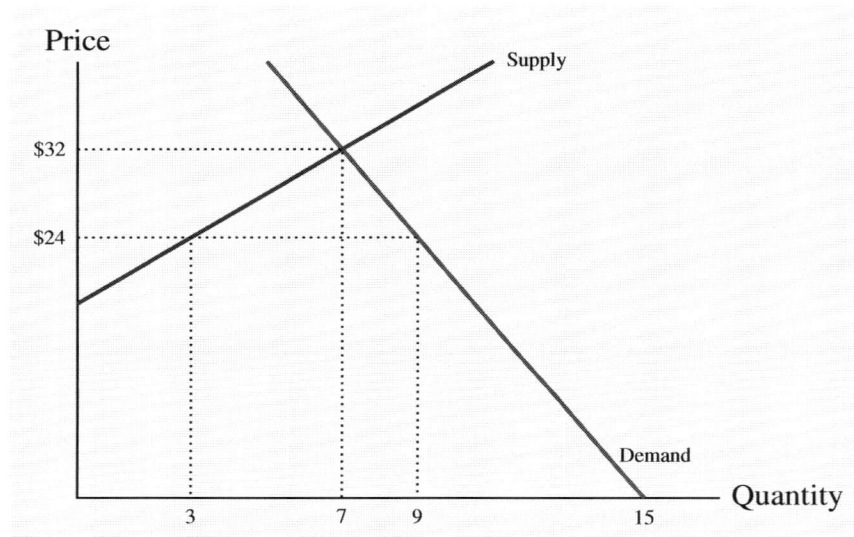

Exercise 3.2.

(a) Demand curve facing *Air Canada* shifts left and down. The price of the substitute *Via Rail* has fallen and reduced the quantity of air transport services demanded at any price.

(b) Demand curve facing *Air Canada* shifts left and down. The substitute car travel has improved in quality and perhaps declined in cost.

(c) Demand curve facing *Air Canada* shifts left and down. A new budget air carrier is another substitute for *Air Canada* that will divide the market for air transport.

Exercise 3.3. The market diagrams are drawn on the assumption that each product can be purchased for a given price, the supply curve in each market segment is horizontal. A downward sloping demand should characterize each market. If the cigarette market is 'quashed' the demand in the market for chewing tobacco, a substitute, should shift outward, leading to higher consumption at the same price.

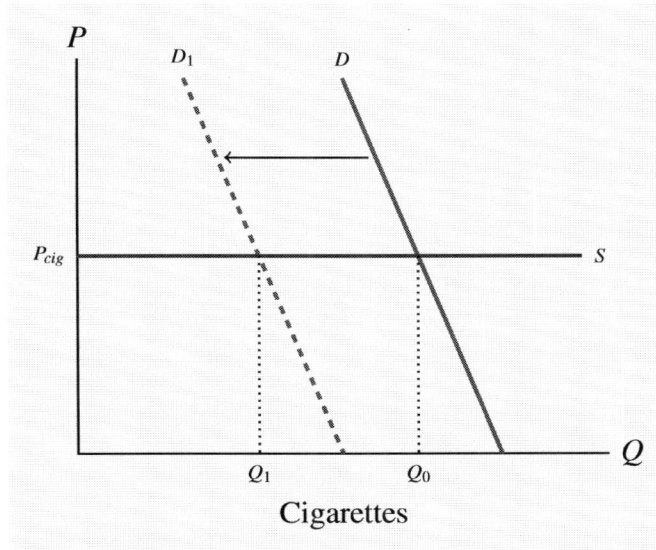

Cigarettes

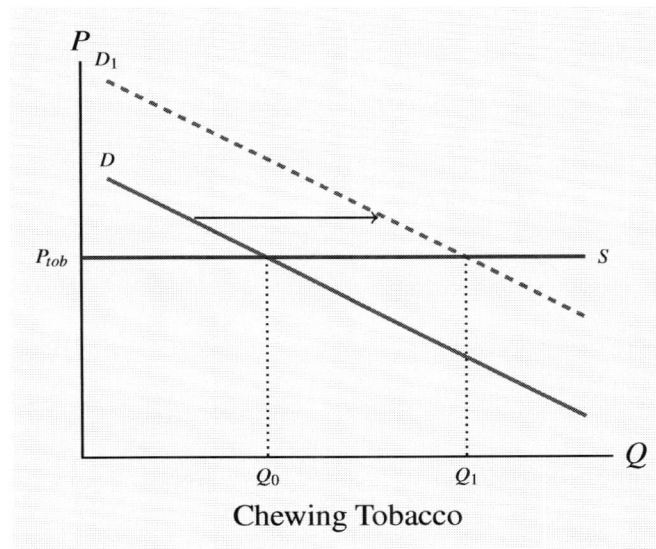

Chewing Tobacco

Exercise 3.4. The supply curve shifts down and parallel, the demand curve shifts up and parallel.

(a) Setting the new supply equal to the new demand: $10 + 2Q = 76 - 4Q$ implies $6Q = 66$ and therefore $Q = 11$, $P = 32$.

Exercise 3.5. The diagram shows that equilibrium quantity is 240, equilibrium price is $130, which are the values obtained from equating supply and demand. At a price of $120 the quantity demanded is 300 and the quantity supplied 210. Excess demand is therefore 90.

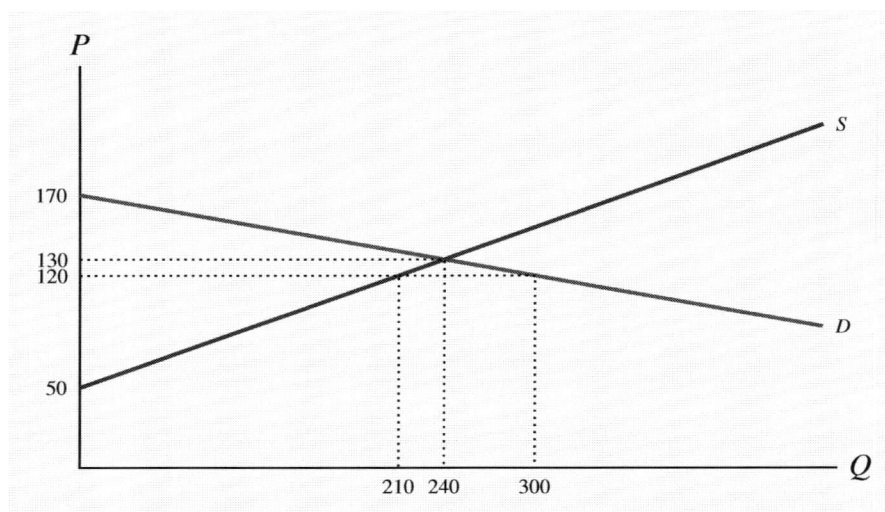

Exercise 3.6.

(a) At a price of $140 quantity demanded is 180 and quantity supplied is 270; excess supply is therefore 90.

(b) Total quotas of 180 will maintain a price of $140. This is obtained by substituting the price of $140 into the demand curve and solving for Q.

Exercise 3.7. It must buy 90 units at a cost of $140 each. Hence it incurs a loss on each unit of $60, making for a total loss of $5,400.

Exercise 3.8.

(a) The quantity axis intercepts are 84 and 126.

(b) The quantities demanded are 160, 110 and 60 respectively, on the market demand curve in the diagram. These values are obtained by solving the quantity demanded in each demand equation for a given price and summing the quantities.

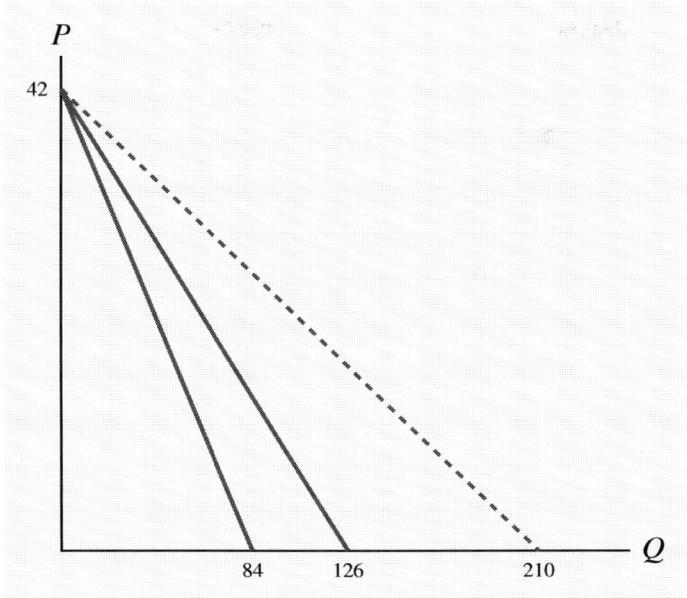

Exercise 3.9.

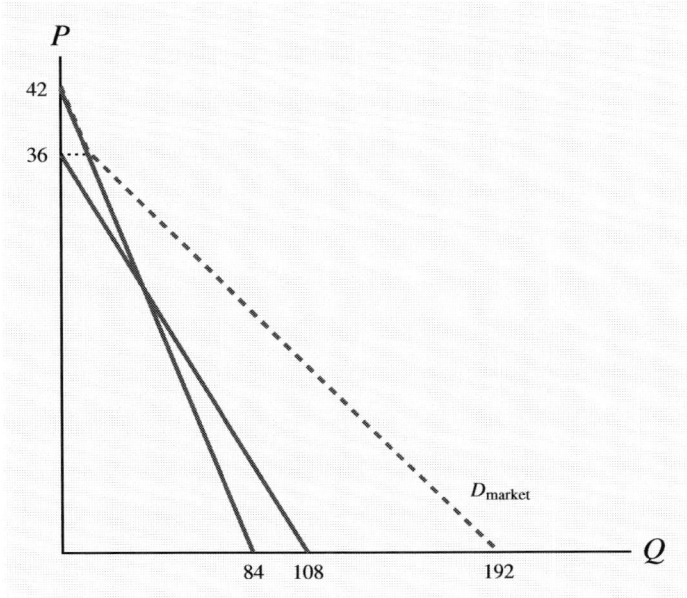

Exercise 3.10.

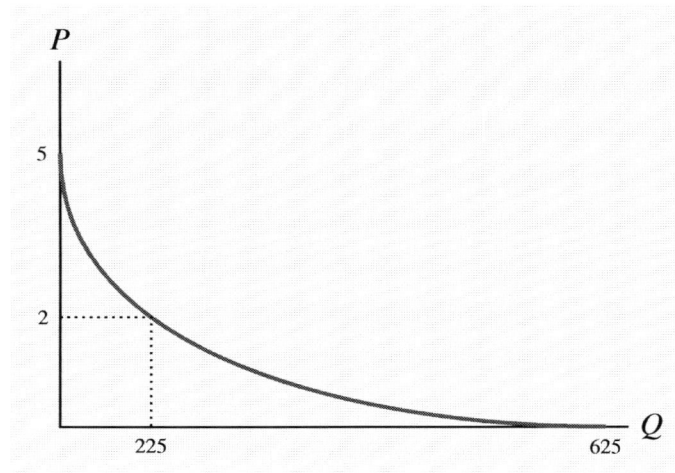

Exercise 3.11.

(a) The equilibrium admission price is $P = \$21$, $TR = \$630$.

(b) The equilibrium price would now become $18 and $TR = \$648$. Yes.

(c) The answer is no, because total revenue falls.

Exercise 3.12. Wages are a cost of bringing lettuce to market. In the market diagram the supply curve for lettuce shifts upwards to reflect the increased costs. If demand is unchanged the price of lettuce rises from P_0 to P_1 and the quantity demanded falls from Q_0 to Q_1.

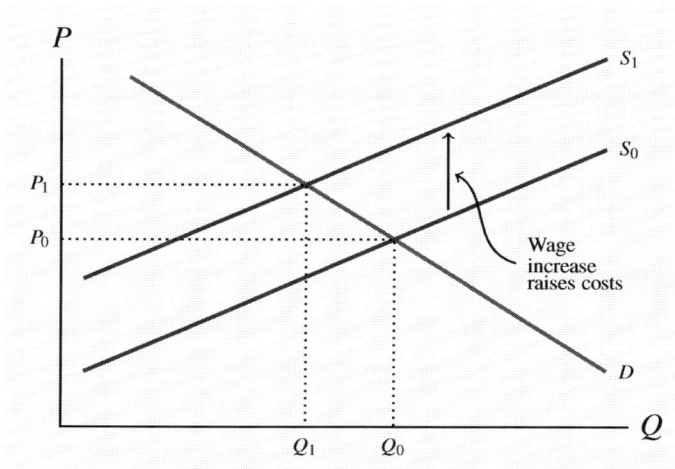

Solutions to exercises for Chapter 4

Exercise 4.1.

(a) Rates of growth of real GDP:

$$2010\text{-}11: \left(\frac{1307}{1282} - 1\right) \times 100\% = 1.95\%, 2011\text{-}12: -1.45\%$$

(b) Rates of inflation:

$$2011: \left(\frac{111.9}{109.1} - 1\right) \times 100\% = 2.7\%, 2012: 24.1\%$$

(c) Rates of growth of labour force and employment:

2010-2011:

Labour: $\left(\dfrac{17.857}{17.593} - 1\right) \times 100\% = 1.5\%$, Employ: $\left(\dfrac{16.696}{16.573} - 1\right) \times 100\% = 0.95\%$

2011-2012:

Labour: 1.5%, Employ: 0.96%

(d) Unemployment rates 2010-2012:

$$2010: \left(\frac{17.593 - 16.537}{17.593}\right) \times 100\% = 6.0\%$$

$$2011: 6.5\%$$

$$2012: 7.0\%$$

Unemployment increased in 2011 and 2012 because the growth in employment was less than the growth in the labour force.

Exercise 4.2.

(a) The participation and employment rates in 2012 were:

$$\left(\frac{18.125}{27.885}\right) \times 100\% = 65\% \text{ and } \left(\frac{16.856}{27.885}\right) \times 100\% = 60.4\%$$

(b) The labour force would decline to $(0.645 \times 27.885) = 17.986$ without any change in employment. As a result the unemployment rate in 2012 would fall to 6.3% but the employment rate would be unchanged. The fall in the participation rate lowers the size of the labour force. The population and employment, and the employment rate are unchanged.

Exercise 4.3. Value added is the difference between the market value of final output and the costs of intermediate inputs to production. In this case the market value of final output is $1,000, the cost of inputs is $625, i.e. ($350 + $125 + $150), and value added is $375 ($1,000 − $625). If brewers wholesale some of their output it is an intermediate input to the service provided by pubs and is not counted in GDP.

Exercise 4.4. Nominal GDP is the market value of final goods and services produced in the economy. The value of final goods produced by the goods industry is $4,000, $5,000 − $1000 sold as intermediate inputs to the service industries. The value of final services produced by the service industries is $9,000, $10,000 − $1,000 sold as intermediate inputs to the goods producing industries. Nominal GDP is $13,000, i.e. $4,000 + $9,000.

The value of output is the sum of value added in the goods and service industries, namely

i. Value added in services= $10,000 − $1,000 intermediate inputs of computers, paper etc.= $9000.

ii. Value added in goods= $5,000 − $1,000 intermediate financial and other services= $4,000.

iii. Value of aggregate output= $13,000.

Exercise 4.5.

(a) Nominal GDP by expenditures= $C + I + G + X − IM = 4,000$.

(b) Net domestic income=Employ income+Business income+invest income= 3650.

(c) Nominal GDP by income=Net domestic income+capital consumption allowance+net indirect taxes= 4,000.

Exercise 4.6.

(a) Investment expenditure is $Y − (C + G + NX) = \$2,000 − (\$1,700 + \$50 + \$40) = \$210$.

(b) If exports are $350 and net exports are $40 imports are $310.

(c) Net domestic income is $GDP − (CCA + T_{in}) = \$1,770$.

(d) Yes. Net exports would be negative if imports exceed exports.

Exercise 4.7.

(a) Growth in nominal GDP from 2012 to 2013 is 10%.

(b) Real GDP in 2012 was $721.15. Real GDP in 2013 was $736.60. Real GDP grew by 2.14%.

(c) Per capita real GDP was $28.8 thousand in 2012 and $24.5 thousand in 2013.

(d) The standard of living declined because population grew faster than real GDP.

Solutions to exercises for Chapter 5

Exercise 5.1.

(a) The AD and AS curves are as shown below.

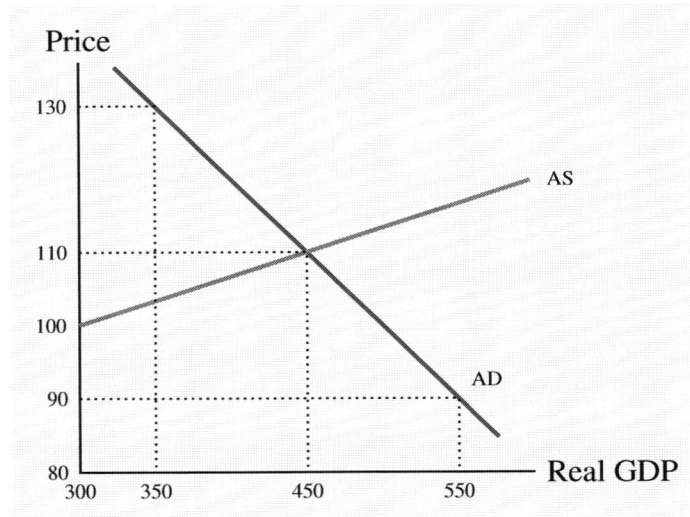

(b) The short run equilibrium values are $P = 110$, $Y = 450$, where the AD and AS curves intersect.

Exercise 5.2.

(a) The diagram shows potential output of $Y_P = 500$ added to the diagram.

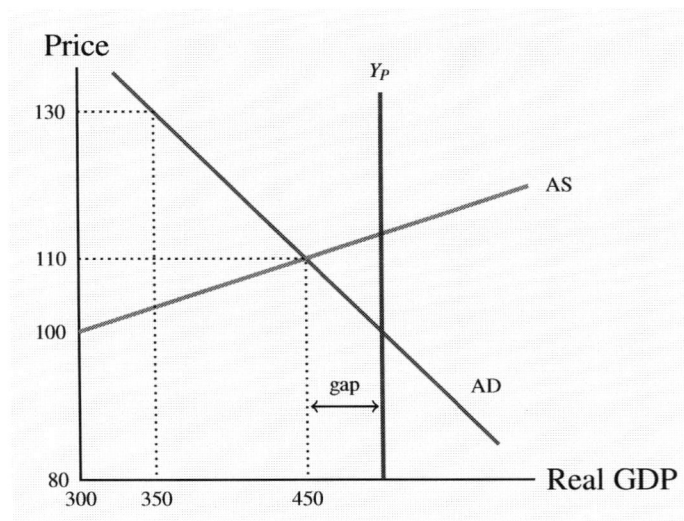

(b) The diagram shows an output gap. Equilibrium $Y \neq Y_P$.

(c) The output gap is $Y - Y_P = (450 - 500) = -50$.

Exercise 5.3. Growth in labour force, or the stock of capital, or improvements in technology that increased the productivity of labour and capital would increase the economy's capacity to produce goods and services and increase potential GDP. As shown in the diagram below, the vertical line measuring potential output would shift to the right. Without an increase in AD a recessionary gap opens. The economy could produce more output at any price level without putting upward pressure on the price level beyond the initial level P_0.

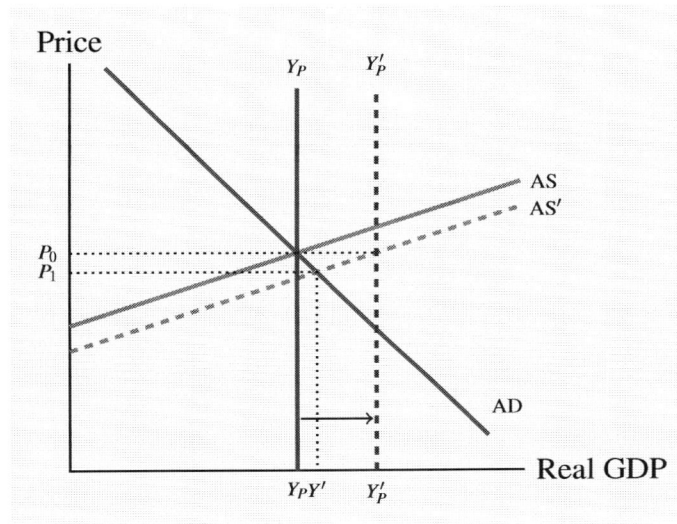

Exercise 5.4.

(a) Short run equilibrium means AD=AS. For the aggregate demand and supply functions given:

$$Y = 2250 - 10 \times (125 + 0.1Y)$$
$$2Y = 2250 - 1250$$
$$Y = 500$$

When $Y = 500$, AS gives $P = 125 + 0.1 \times 500 = 175$.

(b) In the diagram, the intercepts of the AD curve are $Y = 2250$, $P = 225$. The vertical intercept of the AS curve is $P = 125$.

(c) The new AS' curve as shown by the dotted line would be $P = 130 + 0.1Y$, and the AD curve would be $Y = 2250 - 10P$. The new equilibrium value of Y would be lower and P would be higher, namely $Y' = 475$ and $P = 177.5$.

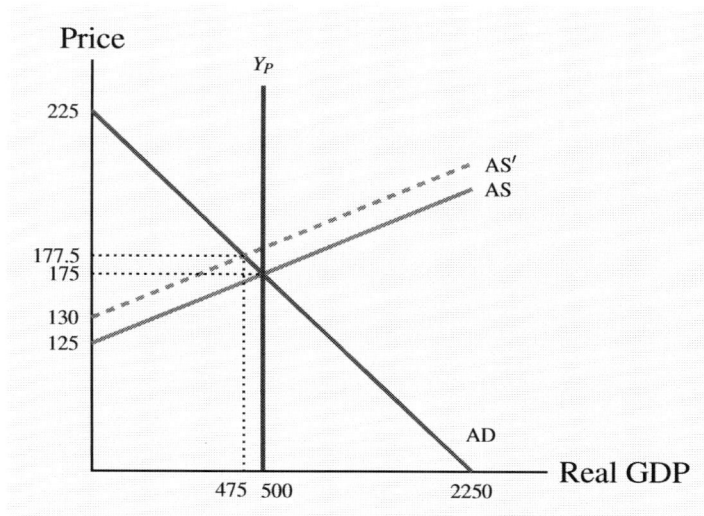

(d) The new AS′ curve is shown as a dotted line in the diagram. There is a recessionary gap of 25.

Exercise 5.5.

(a) A simple approximation of the annual growth in potential output is the sum of the growth in labour force and labour productivity, namely $1.5\% + 1.0\% = 2.5\%$. However it is more accurate to recognize the compounding effect and multiply $1.015 \times 1.01 = 1.0252$, which gives an annual rate of growth of potential output as 2.52%.

(b) The growth in potential output is illustrated by a rightward shift in the Y_P and AS curves as shown below.

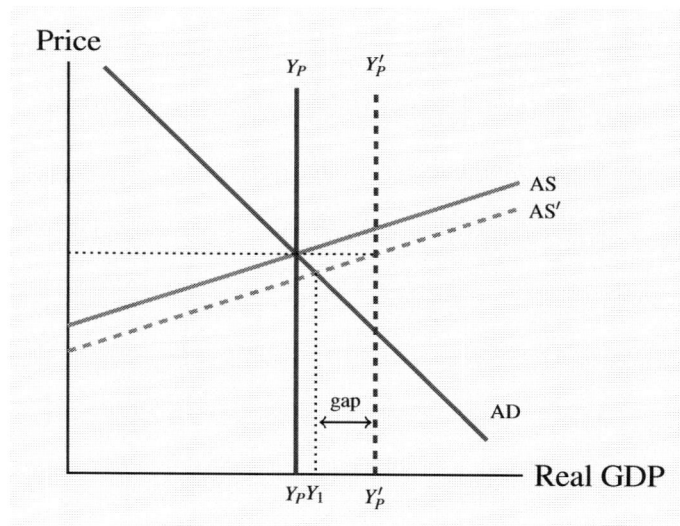

Exercise 5.6. Output gaps in a growing economy are calculated as: $\frac{Y - Y_P}{Y_P} \times 100\%$. The data give the following annual gaps:

Year	2006	2007	2008	2009	2010	2011	2012	2013
Gap	−2.0	−3.6	0	+2.3	−2.5	−6.1	−4.2	−8.9

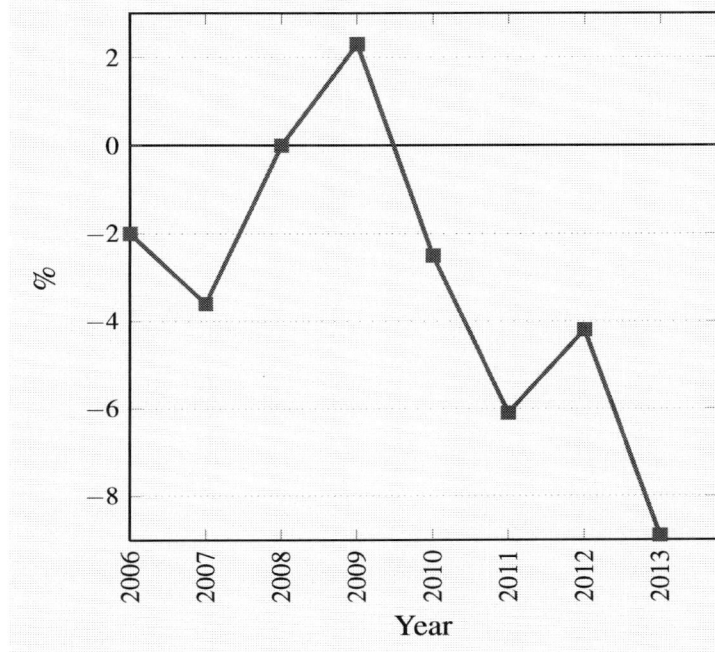

The plot of the output gaps shows the economy in recession in 2006-07, followed by recovery and boom from 2008-09, followed by recession starting in 2010, running into 2011 and then moderating in 2012 before deepening in 2013.

Exercise 5.7. With the output function $Y = 100N$, employment is proportional to output. A 1.0 percent reduction in output (Y) would reduce employment by 1.0 percent.

Solutions to exercises for Chapter 6

Exercise 6.1.

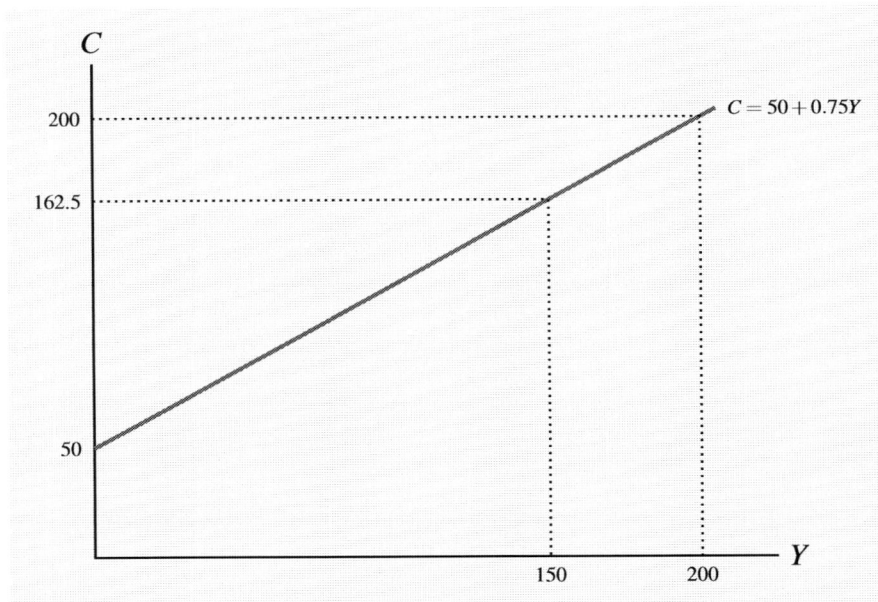

(a) When $Y = 150$, $C = 50 + 0.75 \times 150 = 162.5$.

(b) When $Y = 200$, $C = 50 + 0.75 \times 200 = 200$. The change in consumption caused by the change in income of $50 = \Delta C = 0.75 \times \Delta Y = 37.5$.

(c) If $C = 50 + 0.75Y$, then $S = Y - C = -50 + 0.25Y$.

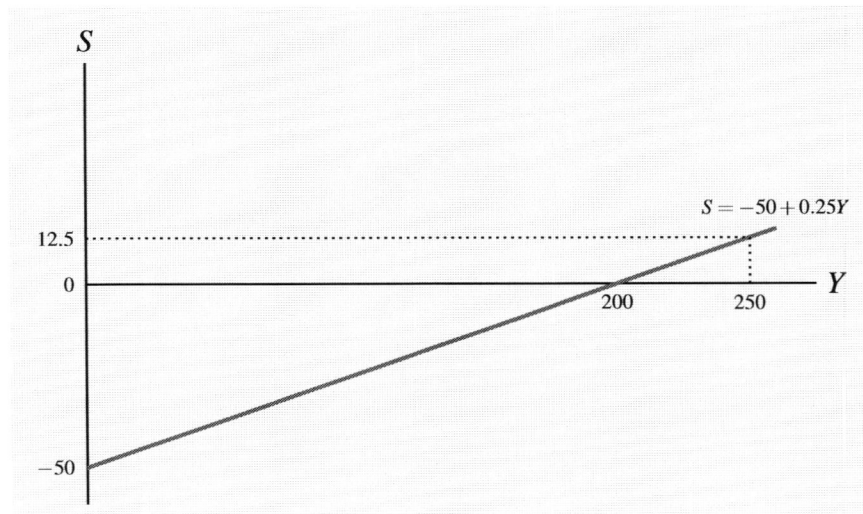

(d) In the diagram in part (c), $S = 0$ when $Y = 200$. If Y increased to 250, saving would increase by: $\Delta S = 0.25 \times 50 = 12.5$.

Exercise 6.2.

(a) A reduction in autonomous expenditure from 50 to 30 would cause a parallel downward shift in the consumption function, and a parallel upward shift in the savings function. The new intercepts with the vertical axes would be 30 and -30 respectively. The slopes are not changed.

(b) The marginal propensity to consume would be lower and the marginal propensity to save higher. The slope of the consumption function would be reduced and that of the saving function increased.

Exercise 6.3.

(a) The AE function is $AE = 105 + 0.5Y$. In the diagram the intercept on the vertical axis is 105 and the slope of AE is 0.5.

(b) The aggregate expenditure function $AE = 105 + 0.5Y$ has an intercept on the vertical axis of 105. This measures autonomous expenditure.

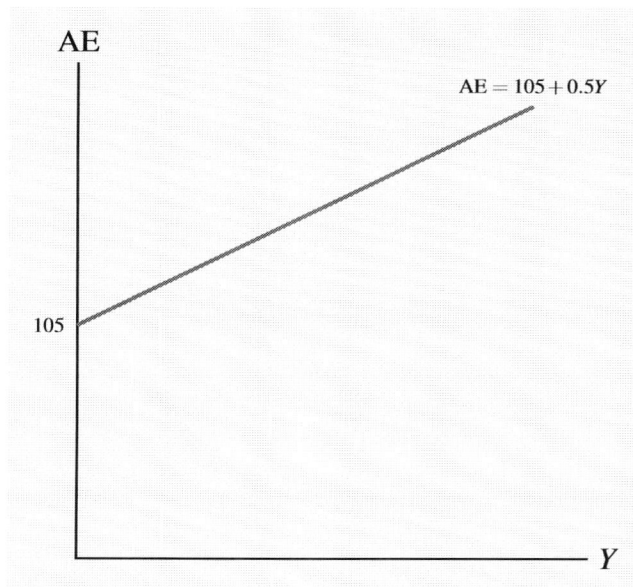

(c) The slope of the AE function is 0.5. It measures the change in AE caused by a change in national income.

Exercise 6.4.

(a) The aggregate expenditure function is $AE = C + I + X - IM$. In this example:

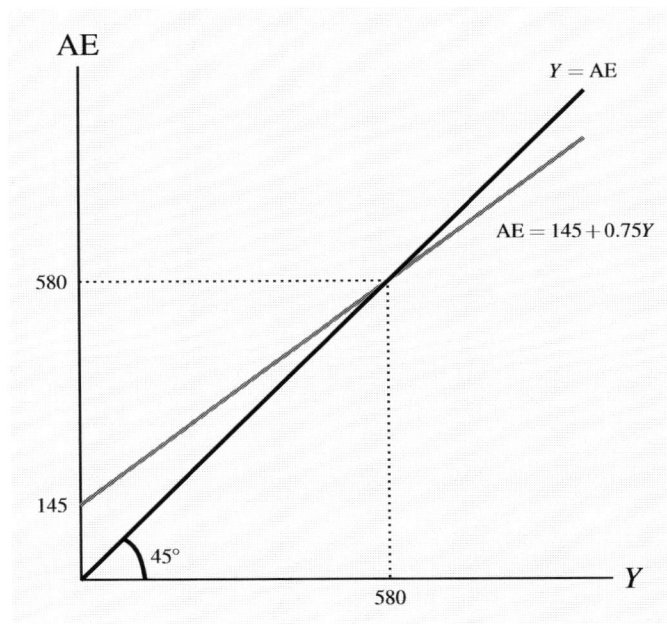

(b) The 45° line is shown in the diagram.

(c) Algebraically, in equilibrium:

$$Y = AE$$
$$Y = 145 + 0.75Y$$
$$Y - 0.75Y = 145$$
$$0.25Y = 145$$
$$Y = 580$$

Exercise 6.5.

(a) If output is OG, planned expenditure would be OB. Planned expenditure would be greater than current output.

(b) At output OG the *unplanned decrease* in inventories is AB.

(c) Business firms will respond by increasing output to meet the strong demand for output.

(d) The equilibrium level of output and expenditure is OH=OD.

(e) If output where at OJ, there would be an *unplanned increase* in inventories in the amount EF.

Exercise 6.6.

(a) The initial equilibrium would be at $Y = OG$.

(b) If the marginal propensity to import, m, were to increase the slope of the AE function, which is MPC minus the marginal propensity to import $(c-m)$, would decrease by a corresponding amount and the new AE function would be AJ.

(c) The new equilibrium, based on the AE function AJ, would be $Y = OF$.

(d) If the MPC increased the new AE function would be AL and the new equilibrium would be $Y = OH$.

Exercise 6.7.

(a) When autonomous expenditure $A = 0$, $MPC = 0.8$ and $MPM = 0.1$. The AE function is:

$$AE = (MPC - MPM)Y$$
$$AE = 0.7Y$$

(b) A diagram to illustrate this AE.

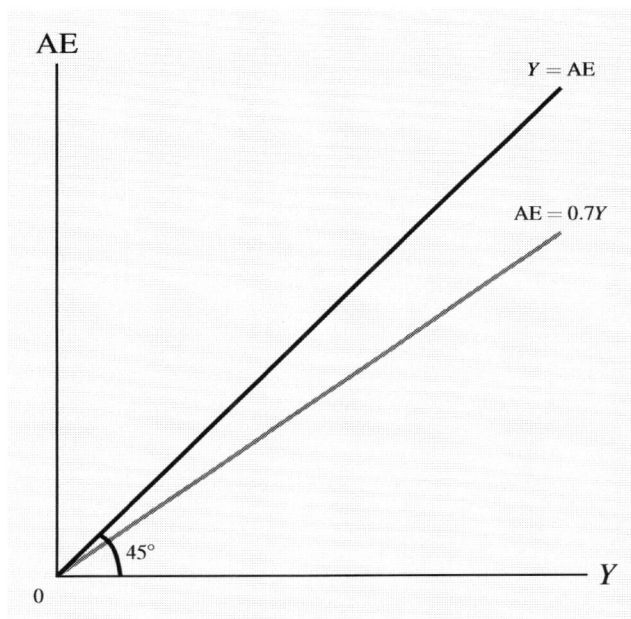

(c) The equilibrium level of real GDP is $Y = 0$.

(d) The equilibrium $Y = 0$ because expenditure is not sufficient to cover the costs of production at any positive level of real GDP.

Exercise 6.8.

(a) The $AE = 105 + 0.5Y$ with $MPC = 0.75$ and $MPM = 0.25$. An increase in investment by 10 with a slope of $AE = 0.5$, increases equilibrium real GDP by: $\Delta I \times$ multiplier $= 20$.

(b) An increase in real GDP by 20 means consumption has increased by 15 and imports have increased by 5 for a net change in induced expenditure by 10.

(c) If the MPC was 0.85 the slope of AE would be $(MPC - MPM = 0.85 - 0.25 = 0.6)$ the increase in investment by 10 would increase equilibrium real GDP by 25, consumption by 21.25 and imports by 6.25 for a net change in induced expenditure of 15. The higher MPC gives a higher slope to AE and a larger multiplier.

Exercise 6.9.

(a) Equilibrium real GDP would be 1,000.

(b) The marginal propensity to consume is $\Delta C / \Delta Y = 0.9$, to import $\Delta IM / \Delta Y = 0.15$.

(c) The multiplier$= 1/(1 - $ slope of AE$)$, the slope of AE is the $MPC - MPM = 0.75$, the multiplier is $1/(1 - 0.75) = 4$.

(d) If actual real GDP were 900, AE would be $250 + 0.75(900) = 925$. If AE is greater than Y inventories are reduced to fill the gap. Planned investment, including planned inventory investment is 100 but the unplanned reduction in inventories reduces actual investment to 75.

(e) An increase in planned investment by 50 with a multiplier of 4 increases equilibrium income and real GDP by 200 to 1,200.

Exercise 6.10. In equilibrium $S + IM = I + X$, which in this case gives: $0.5Y = 150$.

(a) The diagram shows equilibrium income $Y = 300$.

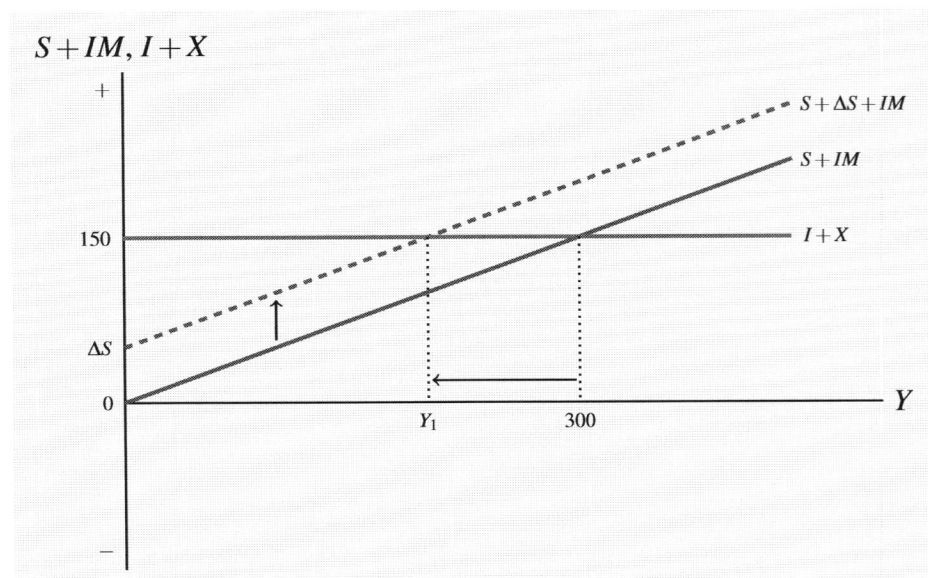

(b) Higher autonomous household saving, which means equally lower autonomous consumption expenditure would lower equilibrium real GDP and income by the increase in saving multiplied by the multiplier.

In the diagram the $S+IM$ line shifts up as shown by the amount of the increase in autonomous saving. Equilibrium real GDP is reduced, but the sums of saving plus imports and investment plus exports are unchanged.

Exercise 6.11.

(a) The AE function $AE = 0.75Y$ is shown in the diagram.

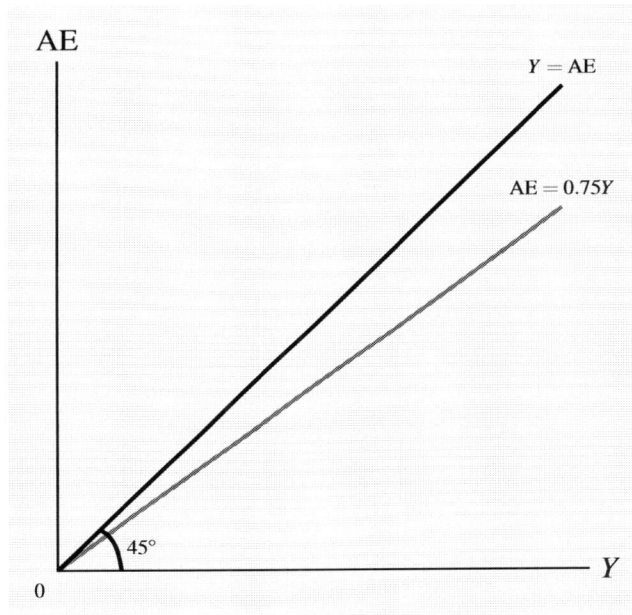

(b) The equilibrium real GDP is $Y = 0$.

$$Y = AE$$
$$Y = 0.75Y$$
$$0.25Y = 0$$
$$Y = 0$$

(c) Equilibrium $Y = 0$ because AE is never sufficient to give producers the revenue they need to cover their costs of production.

Solutions to exercises for Chapter 7

Exercise 7.1. Before government is established $G = 0$, $C_0 + I_0 + NX_0 = 200$ and an $MPC = 0.75$ and $MPM = 0.15$ the aggregate expenditure function is:

$$AE = 200 + 0.6Y$$

Then for equilibrium:

$$Y = AE$$
$$Y = 200 + 0.6Y$$
$$Y_0 = \frac{200}{1 - 0.6} = 500$$

After government is established and $G = 100$: $AE = 300 + 0.6Y$. Equilibrium $Y = Y_1 = 750$.

Exercise 7.2.

(a) The slope of AE in Exercise 7.1 is 0.6. The slope of AE in Exercise 7.2 is 0.525.

(b) The multiplier in Exercise 7.1 is 2.5. The multiplier in Exercise 7.2 is 2.11.

(c) With a tax rate $t = 0.1$ disposable income would be $Y_d = 0.9Y$ giving $AE = 300 + 0.525Y$ and equilibrium $Y = 632$, compared to the equilibrium of 750 in Exercise 7.1.

Exercise 7.3.

(a) The table values are as follows:

Y	$NT = tY$	G	$BB = NT - G$
100	20	100	−80
200	40	100	−60
300	60	100	−40
400	80	100	−20
500	100	100	0
600	120	100	+20
700	140	100	+40

(b) The NT function has an intercept of 0 because there is no autonomous tax revenue, and a slope of 0.2. The G function has a vertical intercept at 100 and zero slope because G is autonomous.

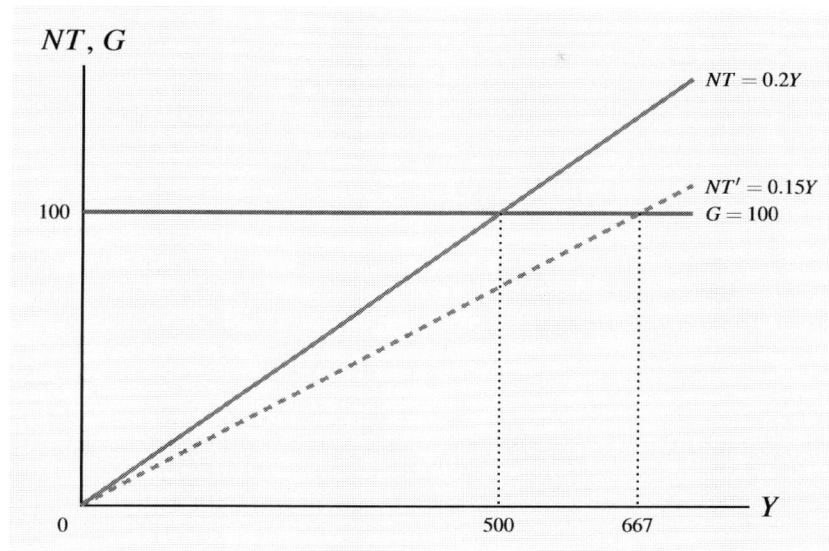

(c) A cut in the net tax rate from $t = 0.20$ to $t = 0.15$ reduces tax revenue proportionately at every level of Y as shown by the lower slope on the tax function NT' in the diagram. The budget balance $NT - G$ is correspondingly lower at every Y.

Exercise 7.4.

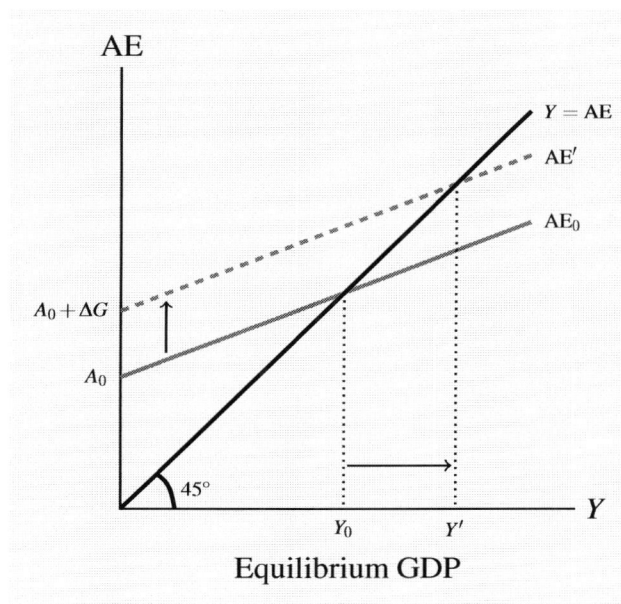

Equilibrium GDP

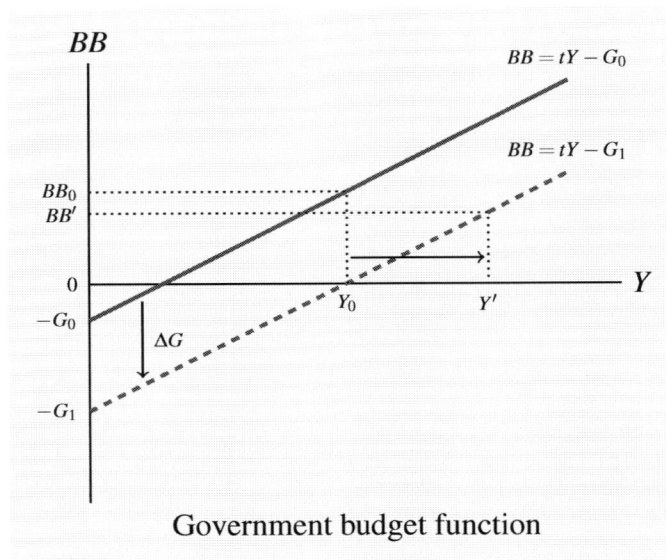

Government budget function

Before the increase in G, equilibrium is $Y = Y_0$ and the government's budget balance is BB_0. The increase in G shifts AE up and the BB function down. The increase in Y combined with the new budget function $BB = tY - G_1$ give a new budget balance BB', smaller than the initial balance, but not reduced by the full amount of the increase in G because the expansionary effect of increased G raised Y and tax revenue.

Exercise 7.5.

(a) The slope of AE is the change in C minus the change in IM caused by a change in real income Y.

$$AE/\Delta Y = MPC \times (1 - t) - m = (0.8 \times 0.75) - 0.15 = 0.45$$

and the multiplier $\Delta Y / \Delta A = [1/(1 - 0.45)] = 1.82$.

(b) Autonomous expenditure is $300 + 400 = 700$. Equilibrium real GDP is autonomous expenditure times the multiplier:

$$Y = 700 \times 1.82 = 1,274$$

With equilibrium income 1,274 the government budget balance, BB, is:

$$BB = tY - G$$
$$= 0.25 \times 1,274 - 400$$
$$= 318.5 - 400$$
$$= -81.5$$

(c) An increase in G by 100 will increase equilibrium Y by 182 and raise tax revenue by 45.5 increasing the government budget deficit to $BB = -136$.

Exercise 7.6.

(a) With $Y = 750$ and $Y_P = 850$ there is a recessionary gap$= Y - Y_P = -100$.

(b) If the $MPC = 0.75$, $MPM = 0.10$ and $t = 0.20$ the slope of AE $= 0.75(1 - 0.20) - 0.1 = 0.5$, and the multiplier is:

$$\frac{1}{1 - 0.5} = 2.0$$

To increase equilibrium income by 100 requires an increase in G by $100/2 = 50$.

(c) With the initial tax rate $t = 0.20$, the $MPC = 0.75$ and $MPM = 0.10$ and $Y = 750$, total autonomous was $750/2 = 375$. The new tax rate needed for equilibrium $Y = 850$ and $A_0 = 375$ must give a multiplier of $850/375 = 2.267$.

Then $\frac{1}{1 - 0.75(1 - t_1) + 0.10} = 2.267$, and solving for t_1 gives $t_1 = 0.121$. As an alternative to increasing G by 50 to eliminate the GDP gap, the government could cut the net tax rate by $0.20 - 0.121 = 0.079$ or close to 40%.

Exercise 7.7.

(a) The vertical intercept of BB is $-G$ and the slope of BB is the net tax rate t.

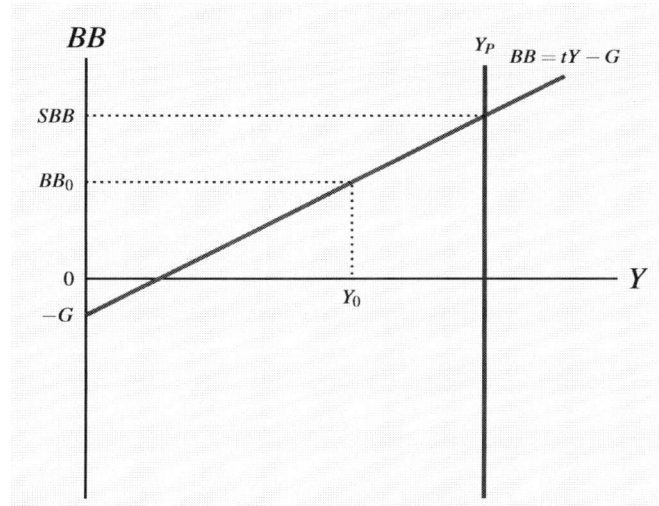

(b) The structural budget balance is shown at SBB, the budget balance at Y_P. If the economy has a recessionary gap as at Y_0 the actual budget balance is BB_0.

(c) Automatic stabilization comes from the slope of the budget function. Changes in Y move the economy along the budget function, causing pro-cyclical changes in the actual budget balance but do not change the structural balance. Discretionary fiscal policy changes t, or G or both t and G. The result is a new budget function and a new structural budget balance.

Exercise 7.8.

(a) With $Y = 2000$ and a public debt of 1000 the debt/GDP ratio is 0.5 or 50%.

(b) After an increase in government expenditure $\Delta G = 10$, equilibrium $Y = 2020$ and the change in the government's budget balance is $\Delta T - \Delta G = 2 - 10 = -8$.

(c) Financing this budget deficit results in a national debt of 1008. The new debt/GDP ratio is $1008/2020 = 49.9\%$.

Solutions to exercises for Chapter 8

Exercise 8.1. Money is anything generally accepted as a means of payment, a store of wealth and a unit of account.

In Canada today, Bank of Canada notes, coins and bank deposits are money.

The money supply is the sum of notes and coin in circulation outside the banking system, and bank deposits.

A debit card is money because, like a cheque, it transfers bank deposits from the bank account of the payer to the bank account of the payee. There is no payment further financial obligation. Using a credit card to make a payment creates a credit card debt for the payer that must be settled by a money payment – notes or bank deposits.

Exercise 8.2. A central bank, like the Bank of Canada works to control money and financial conditions in the economy using its position as monopoly supplier of monetary base – bank reserve assets. It is not profit oriented. It does not attempt to make a profit.

A commercial bank works to earn a profit for its owners (shareholders) buy providing banking services to the non-bank public on terms that generate net interest income. It is profit oriented.

Exercise 8.3. Banks create money by issuing their own deposit liabilities (IOUs) in payment for the assets they buy, such as financial securities and customer loan contracts.

Suppose banks operate to a 5% reserve ratio. $rr = 0.05$.

The following balance sheets show the initial new deposit and the deposit creation that follows.

(a) The new deposit provides the banks with a 100 increase in cash (reserve asset) in exchange for 100 in new deposit liabilities.

All banks			
Assets		Liabilities	
Cash	+100	Deposits	+100

(excess reserves +95)

(b) In part (a) banks hold $95 excess reserves based on the reserve ratio of 5%. In part (b) they make loans equal to their excess reserves $95, and pay for those loans by creating new deposit liabilities, $95.

Assets		Liabilities	
Loans	+95	Deposits	+95

(c) Assuming the public uses bank deposits as money and does not withdraw cash from the banking system, the banks expand their lending and create new deposits to a total of $+1,900$, based on the initial increase in cash reserves and the reserve ratio of 5%. The deposit multiplier is: $\Delta D = \Delta R/rr = 100/0.05 = 2,000$.

Assets		Liabilities	
Cash	+100	Deposits	+2,000
Loans	+1,900		
	+2,000		

Exercise 8.4. If banks have a reserve ratio of $rr = 10\%$ and the public has a currency ratio of $cr = 10\%$ a new cash deposit of $1,000 to the banking system would allow an expansion of bank deposits by:

$$\Delta D = \Delta MB \times [1/(rr + cr)]$$
$$\Delta D = 1,000 \times [1/(0.10 + 0.10)]$$
$$\Delta D = 1,000 \times (1/0.2)$$
$$\Delta D = 5,000$$

Deposit expansion beyond the initial $1,000 would be the result of a $4,000 increase in bank lending.

With an expansion of bank deposits by $5,000 the public would increase cash holdings by $500 (i.e. 10%).

Yes. If the banks could encourage a lower currency ratio a larger share of the monetary base would be available to the banks as reserves to support bank lending and deposit creation. A lower currency ratio increases the deposit and money supply multipliers that and bank lending.

Exercise 8.5. Confidence in the banking system is based partly on the established reputations of banks in converting deposits into cash and the general acceptability of bank deposits as means of payment. This confidence is reinforced by the insurance coverage on deposits up to $100,000 provided by CDIC.

Exercise 8.6. The money multiplier determines the change in the money supply that results from a change in the monetary base. It would be useful to a central bank wishing to control the money supply using its control and management of the monetary base.

Exercise 8.7.

(a) With a monetary base of $MB = 1,000$ a reserve ratio of $rr = 0.10$ and a currency ratio of $cr = 0.15$ the money supply function is:

$$M_S = \frac{1+cr}{rr+cr} \times MB = \frac{1.15}{0.25} \times 100 = 4,600$$

(b) If the monetary base decreased by 100, money supply would decrease by:

$$\Delta M_S = \frac{1+cr}{rr+cr} \times \Delta MB = \frac{1.15}{0.25} \times (-\$100) = -\$460$$

Exercise 8.8. The financial crisis made both banks and the non-bank public more concerned about the risks attached to making loans and to holding bank deposits. The banks responded by increasing their reserve ratios and by being more selective about the quality of loans and other assets they bought. Even if total bank assets were not reduced overall some forms of bank credit did dry up and some potential borrowers are denied credit.

Concerns about the stability of banks and other financial institutions led the non-bank public to hold more of their money in cash rather than deposits. If the currency ratio is increased and the banking system's lending capacity is reduced.

The effects of increased reserve ratios and currency ratios are smaller deposit multipliers, reduced bank lending and reduced money supply in the absence of an offsetting increase in the monetary base.

Exercise 8.9. With monetary base $H = \$1,000$, $rr = 0.05$ and $cr = 0.10$ the money supply would be:

$$M = 1,000 \times \left(\frac{1+0.10}{0.05+0.10} \right) = 1,000 \times 7.33 = 7,333.33$$

This money supply is shown by the vertical line M in the diagram.

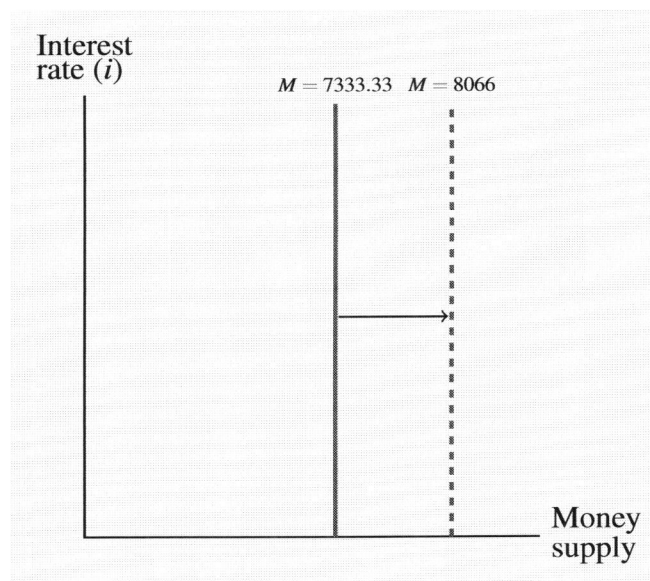

If high powered money were to increase by 10 percent to 1,100 the money supply would be increased by 733 to 8,066. The money supply function in the diagram is shifted to the right to show this effect.

Exercise 8.10. If the *cr* falls as interest rates rise the money multiplier would increase as interest rates increased giving a positive relationship between the interest rate and the money supply.

The diagram shows a money supply function with $\Delta M / \Delta i > 0$.

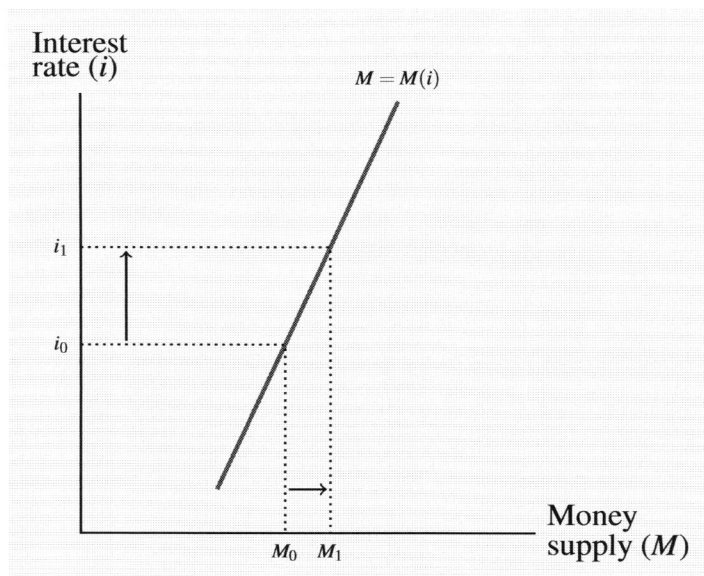

Solutions to exercises for Chapter 9

Exercise 9.1. A perpetual bond with a 3% coupon would have a market price of $100 if the current market rate were 3%. (Yield=coupon/price. Price=coupon/yield= $3.00/0.03 = $100).

Exercise 9.2.

(a) The market price of the bond is the present value of the future stream of payments it provides. A two-year 5% bond, when market rates are 4% has a present value of:

$$P_B = PV = \frac{\$5}{1.04} + \frac{\$105}{(1.04)^2} = \$4.81 + \$97.08 = \$101.89$$

(b) If market rates rise to 6%, then the market price of the two-year 5% bond will be:

$$P_B = PV = \frac{\$5}{1.06} + \frac{\$105}{(1.06)^2} = \$4.72 + \$93.45 = \$98.17$$

(c) The market risk in holding bonds is that bond prices and interest rates vary inversely. A rise in market interest rates means a fall in bond prices and capital losses for bondholders, at least on paper.

Exercise 9.3. The price of $1,000 three year 6% bond that yields 5.5%, the current market rate, for three year bonds is:

$$P_B = PV = \frac{\$60}{1.055} + \frac{\$60}{(1.055)^2} + \frac{\$1,060}{(1.055)^3} = \$56.87 + \$53.91 + \$902.71 = \$1,013.49$$

Therefore paying $1,015 for the $1,000 bond would be too high a price in terms of current market yields.

Exercise 9.4.

(a) The horizontal intercept in the diagram (below) shows the money balances people would want to hold, based on their income (Y_0) if the interest rate, and thus the opportunity cost of holding money were zero. The slope of the line shows how portfolio managers would adjust their holdings of money (vs bonds) if interest rates were to change.

(b) At the interest rate i_0 the demand for money balances is L_0. Some money balances are held to make regular payments, some to provide for uncertainty in the timing of receipts and payments, and some to lower the risks in portfolios of bonds and money.

(c) If interest rates dropped from i_0 to i_1 in the diagram, the people demand for money balances would increase from L_0 to L_1. Lower interest rates mean lower opportunity costs to holding money balances.

A fall in interest rates increases the demand for money balances and reduces the demand for bonds. Portfolios shift from bonds to money.

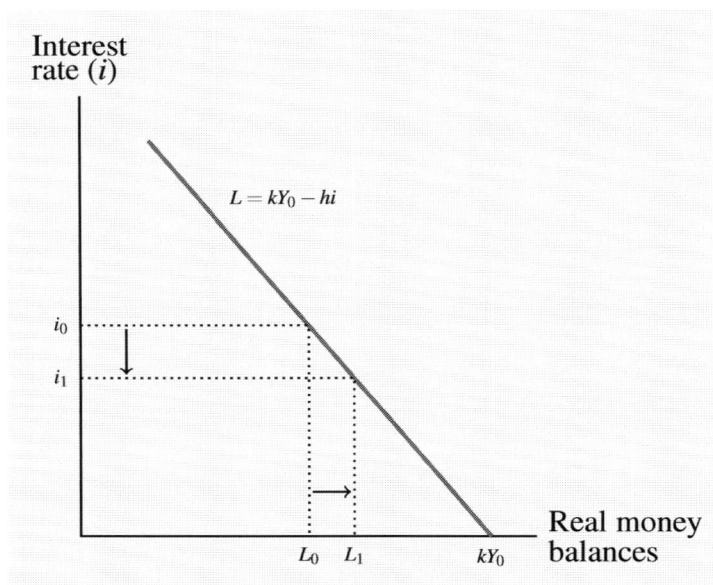

(d) An increase in real GDP ($\Delta Y > 0$) would shift the demand for money function to the right by the amount $k\Delta Y$. Higher Y means higher income and expenditure levels and a need for larger transaction balances to make payments.

Exercise 9.5.

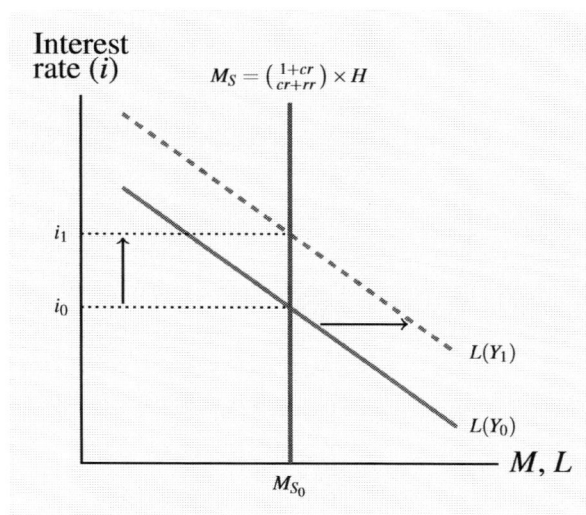

In the diagram the M_S line is vertical. M_S is not affected by interest rates. The monetary base and the money multiplier determine the position of the M_S line. The position of the demand for money function L is determined by the level of real income Y_0, and the transactions demand kY_0. The slope of the L function illustrates the reaction of portfolio managers, changing the mix of money and bonds in portfolios in response to changes in interest rates. Higher interest rates reduce the demand for money balances and increase the demand for bonds.

(a) An increase in income to Y_1 shifts the demand for money function L to the right to $L(Y_1)$. The excess demand for money balances at the initial interest rate i_0 results in the sale of bonds, bond prices fall and yields increase until interest rates rise to i_1.

(b) With higher Y and higher demand for money the new equilibrium interest rate is higher but money holdings are unchanged because the money supply is fixed.

Exercise 9.6. A fall in Canadian interest rates relative to euro rates makes euro bonds more attractive to portfolio managers than Canadian bonds. Reduced demand for Canadian bonds by foreign bondholders reduces the supply of euros on the market while increased demand for euro bonds by Canadian bondholders increases the demand for euros. The diagram shows these changes in supply and demand and the rise in the exchange rate that result.

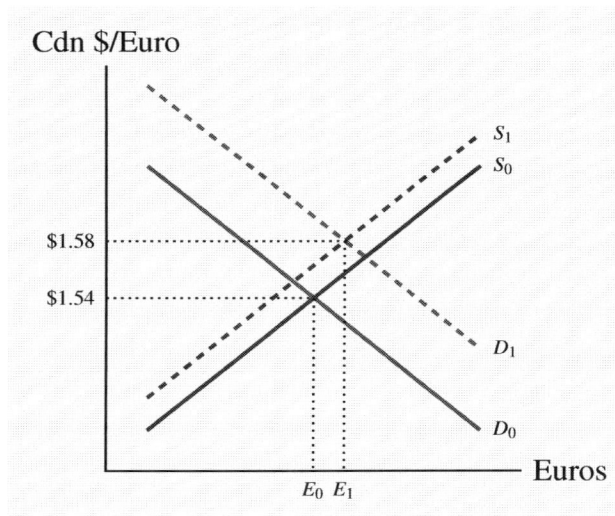

Exercise 9.7.

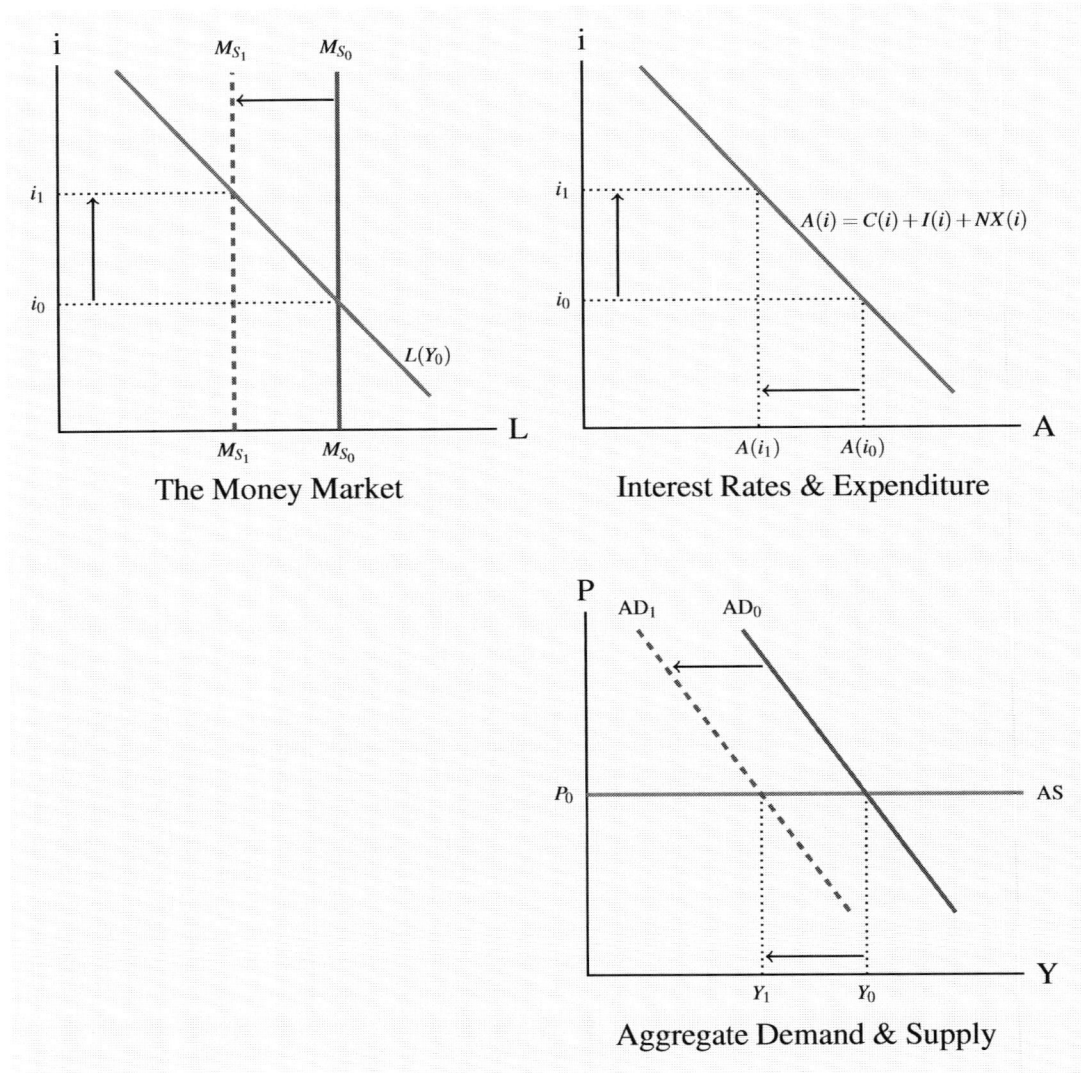

The Money Market

Interest Rates & Expenditure

Aggregate Demand & Supply

(a) A reduction in M_S shifts the M_S line to the left, raising interest rates and lowering expenditure to $A(i_1)$. AD shifts to the left by the change in A times the multiplier to AD_1 and Y is reduced to Y_1.

(b) Alternatively, an increase in precautionary demand for money would shift the demand for money (L) to the right, raising interest rates and lowering expenditure and aggregate demand and equilibrium Y.

(c) Alternatively, any increase in autonomous expenditure would shift the expenditure function to the right, the AD function to the right and higher Y would increase the demand for money balances L. as a result interest rates would rise offsetting some of the increase in investment expenditure (moving along the $A(r)$ function) and shifting AD back to the left. The net result would be a increase in investment, interest rates and equilibrium Y.

Solutions to exercises for Chapter 10

Exercise 10.1. A central bank that operated to make maximum profits would cause financial market instability by expanding the monetary base through its purchase of interest bearing government bonds until the yields on those bonds were driven to (approximately) zero.

A commercial bank pursues profits as long as the costs of raising funds through deposit expansion are less than the interest revenue earned by expanding its lending. The bank's shareholders expect a positive return on their equity in the business. Competition among banks and the public's concern about the solvency of a bank means the costs of funds rises as the bank expands, thereby eliminating the profitability of further expansion.

Currently, the central bank's operating objective is to control the rate of inflation based on an agreed target inflation rate of 2%.

The central bank's unique position as monopoly supplier of the monetary base, cash and central bank deposits, gives it the power to pursue its monetary policy objectives.

Exercise 10.2. Monetary base, central bank notes (cash) and deposits, are the ultimate means of payment in the economy. Commercial banks issue deposits that are convertible into cash on demand. This convertibility together with the public's demand for cash balances creates a demand for monetary base that limits the size of commercial bank deposit liabilities. The central bank's control of the monetary base gives it control of the money supply and interest rates.

Exercise 10.3. A change in monetary base is by itself a direct change in the money supply. But the profit seeking behaviour of the commercial banks causes a larger change in the money supply as a result of ΔMB. If $\Delta MB > 0$, for example, and the public deposits these new funds in the banks, the banks find they are holding excess reserves. These reserves support an increase in bank lending and the deposit creation that goes with it. The money supply increases based on the money supply multiplier provided the currency and reserve ratios are constant.

Exercise 10.4.

(a) The purchase of $10 million in the open market by the central bank creates $10 million in monetary base, which increase the reserves of the commercial banks, provided it is not held as cash by the non-bank public.

(b) With a reserve ratio $rr = 0.025$ and a cash ratio $cr = 0.075$ a $10 million increase in monetary base results in:

  i. An increase in money supply of $107.5 million.

  ii. An increase in public cash holdings of $7.5 million.

  iii. An increase in bank reserve balances of $2.5 million.

Exercise 10.5. To set and maintain interest rate at i_0 in the diagram the central bank provides whatever money supply is demanded at that interest rate. This is shown in the diagram by the horizontal M_S line at i_0.

An increase in real output from Y_0 to Y_1 would increase the demand for money, shifting the $L(Y)$ line in the diagram to the right to $L(Y_1)$. The money supply would increase to M_{S1} to meet the increased demand for money at the interest rate i_0.

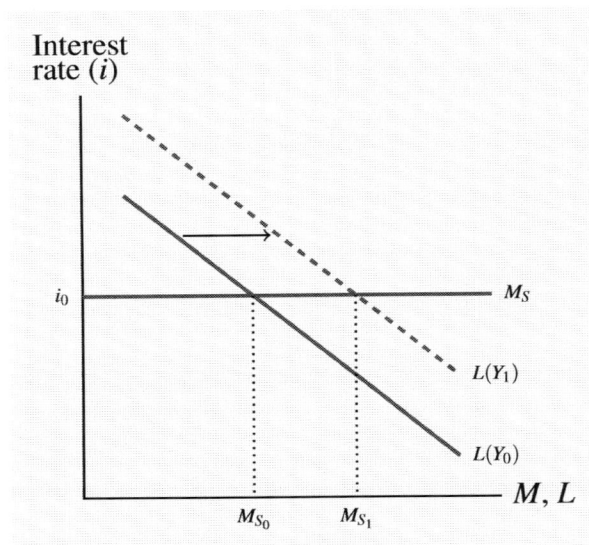

Exercice 10.6.

(a) The Bank of Canada's monetary policy target is an inflation control target of 2% in the CPI within a range of 1%-3%. The Bank aims at a 2% inflation rate over six to eight quarters.

(b) The Bank uses the overnight interest rate as its monetary policy instrument to influence short-term interest rates by raising or lowering the target and operating band it sets for the overnight rate.

(c) Implementing monetary policy by setting the interest rate means the Bank gives up its short-term control of the money supply.

Exercise 10.7. The market for overnight funds:

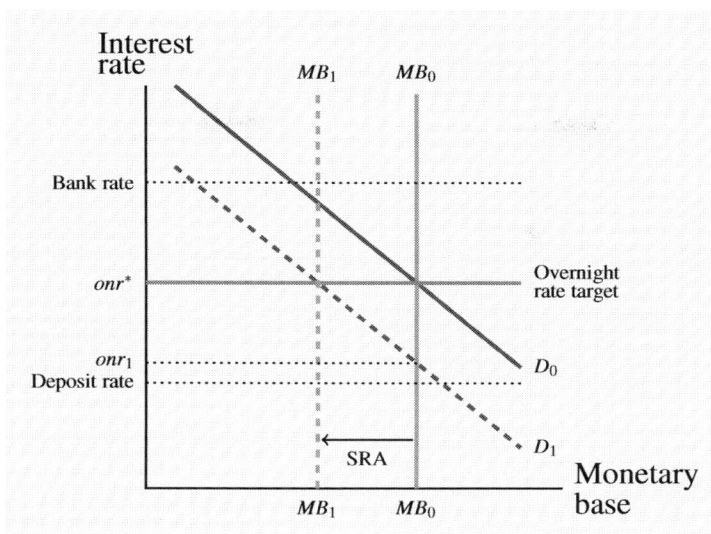

The Bank has set its target for the overnight rate at ONR* consistent with a demand for monetary base D_0. If it happens that the demand for monetary base is less than D_0, for example D_1, the ONR will fall below the Bank's target. To prevent this the Bank can remove some monetary base from the overnight market by selling short term securities to the banks on the agreement that it will buy those securities back the next day. This is a 'sale and repurchase agreement', and SRA. Its effect is to reduce the monetary base, as illustrated by the shift to MB_1, and maintain ONR* as shown by the intersection of D_1 and MB_1.

The Bank uses an SRA rather than an open market operation because an SRA makes an immediate change in the clearing balance position of the banks that last for one day. It is a very short-term adjustment. An open market operation takes time to affect the clearing balance position of the banks as it works its way through bond markets and bank customer accounts to clearing balances. It is better suited to longer term management of the monetary base rather than very short term and likely temporary adjustments to bank clearing balances.

Exercise 10.8.

(a) The central bank chooses and sets the interest rate it thinks will be consistent with equilibrium at potential output at its target rate of inflation.

(b) A rise in the unemployment rate would indicate a fall in aggregate demand and call for a decrease in the Bank's interest rate from its basic setting.

(c) An inflation rate above the Bank's target would indicate stronger than expected aggregate demand and call for a rise in the Bank's interest rate from its basic setting.

(d) A persistent change in either unemployment or inflation would lead the Bank to change its basic interest rate setting.

Exercise 10.9. The Bank's setting of the interest rate i_0 in the left hand diagram gives the AD curve $AD(i_0)$ in the right hand diagram and equilibrium at π^*, Y_P.

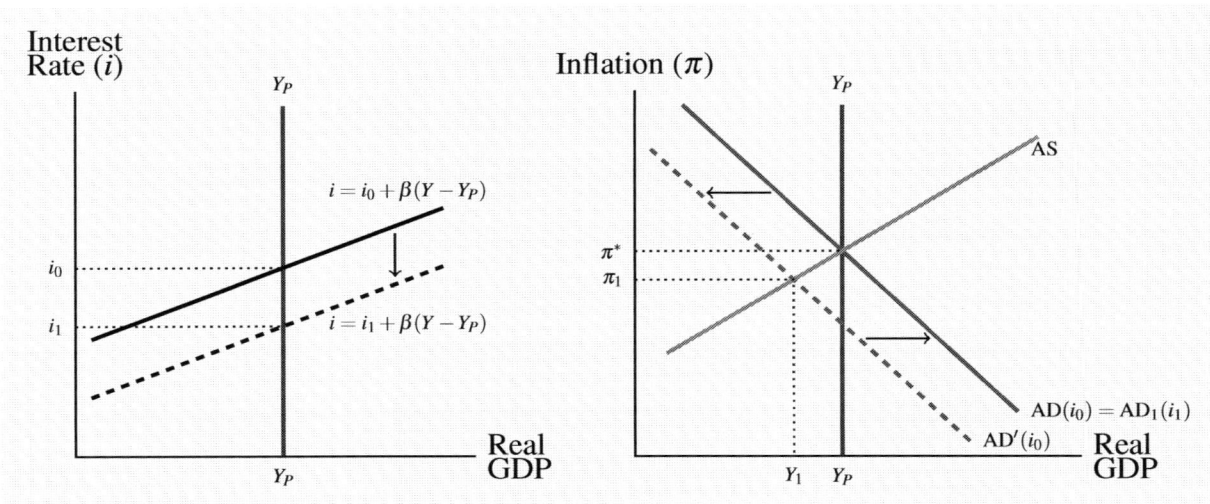

A persistent change in expenditure such as a decrease in investment or net exports would shift the $AD(i_0)$ to $AD'(i_0)$. The inflation rate would fall and output would fall to $Y_1 < Y_P$ in the diagram.

The Bank responds by lowering its interest rate setting to i_1 in the left-hand diagram lowering the monetary policy function. The lower setting for the interest rate shifts $AD'(i_0)$ to $AD'(i_1)$, which coincides with $AD(i_0)$.

The central bank's reaction to the change in AD has stabilized Y at Y_P.

Solutions to exercises for Chapter 11

Exercise 11.1.

(a) The money market diagram illustrates the determination of the equilibrium interest rate i_0 by the real money supply (M_0/P_0) and the demand for real money balances at the income level Y_0, $L(Y_0)$.

An increase in the general price level from P_0 to P_1 reduces the real money supply to M_0/P_1, shifting the money supply function in the diagram to the left and raising the interest rate to i_1. A fall in P would have the opposite effect.

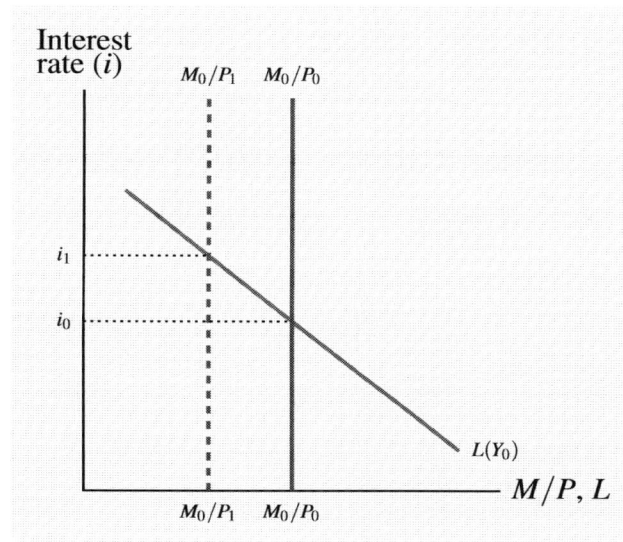

(b) Changes in interest rates shift the AE function. If the initial AE function is $AE(i_0)$, a lower interest rate shifts AE up to $AE(i_2)$. A higher interest rate shifts AE down. Equilibrium real GDP changes as a result of the changes in AE caused by changes in interest rates.

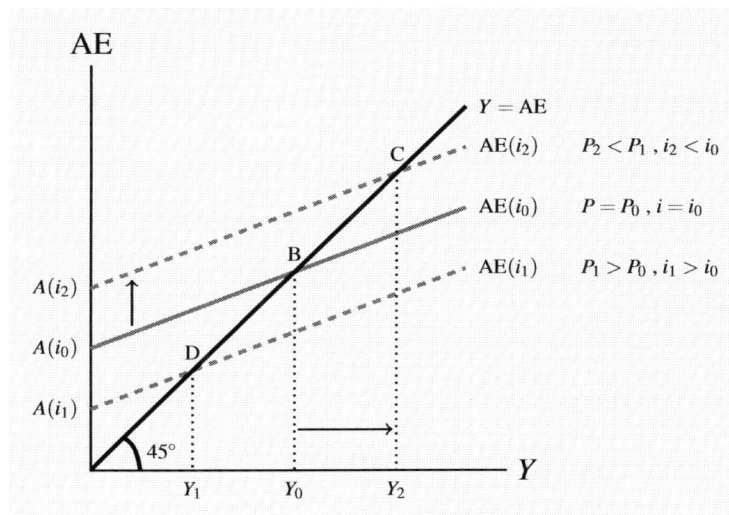

(c) The AD curve is the locus of equilibrium combinations of real GDP (Y) and the general price level (P). Points B, C and D in the above diagram are three such combinations. These combinations plotted in P, Y space give the AD curve for the money supply M_0.

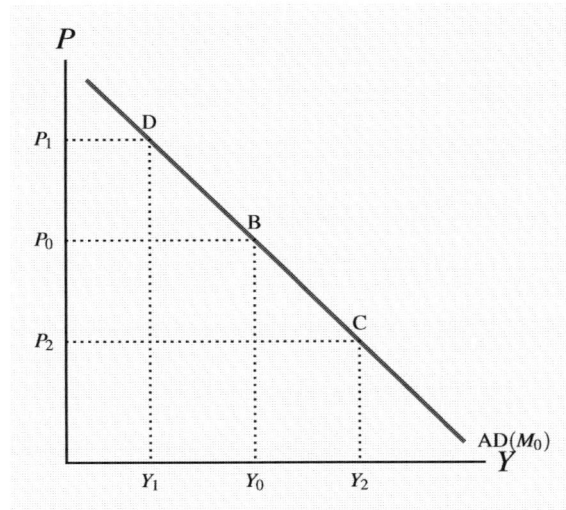

Exercise 11.2. A demand for money that is not very sensitive to interest rate changes (a steep L function) and expenditures that are very sensitive to interest rates (a flat $A(i)$ function) would result in large changes in AE and equilibrium real GDP as a result of changes in P. The following diagrams illustrate.

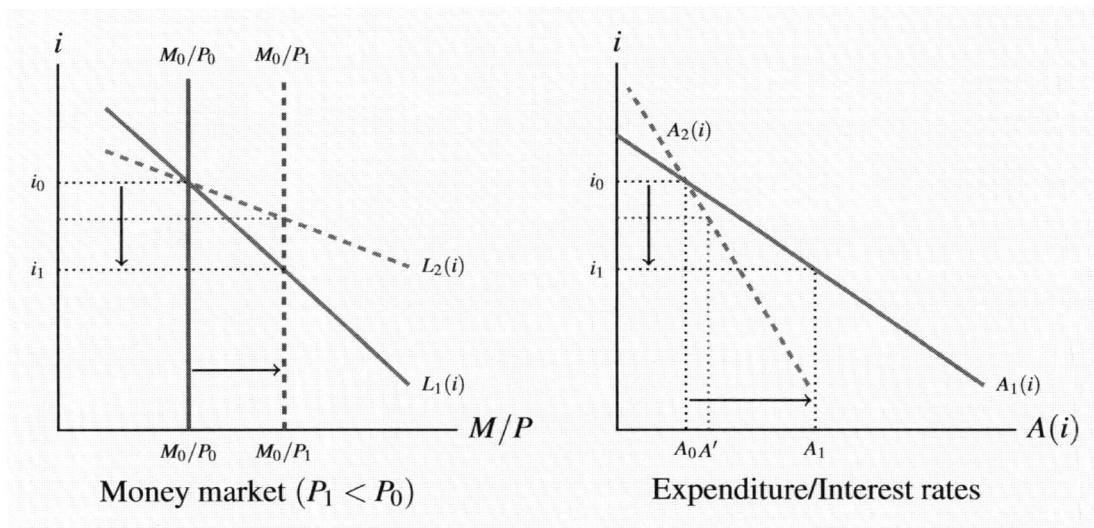

With the demand for money $L_1(i)$, not very sensitive to interest rates, a fall in price from P_0 to P_1 lowers the interest rate to i_1 and with $A_1(i)$, very sensitive to interest rates, autonomous expenditure increases from A_0 to A_1. The effect on AE and equilibrium Y is large compared to the effects of the same fall in prices when the opposite conditions prevail, as illustrated by the money demand $L_2(i)$ and the $A_2(i)$ expenditure function.

Exercise 11.3. A flatter AE curve means a smaller multiplier and smaller changes in real GDP as a result of a change in P that changes interest rates and interest sensitive autonomous expenditure. The slope of the AD curve $- \Delta P / \Delta Y$ is determined by the change in autonomous expenditure $A(i)$ when $\Delta P = \Delta i$ and the change in equilibrium real GDP caused by a change in A, $(\Delta Y / \Delta A)$. $\Delta Y / \Delta A$ is the multiplier, which is $1/(1 - \text{slope AE})$. A flatter AE curve gives a smaller multiplier and thus a smaller ΔY as a result of ΔP. The AD curve is steeper when the slope of the AE curve is lower.

Exercise 11.4.

(a) When $P = 1$, $AE = 200 + 0.5Y$. When $P = 2$, $AE = 150 + 0.5Y$. When $P = 3$, $AE = 133.3 + 0.5Y$.

(b) A rise in P reduced the real money supply, causing a rise in interest rates, lower interest-sensitive expenditure and lower AE at every level of real GDP.

(c) The equilibrium levels of expenditure and real GDP are: $P = 1$, $Y = 400$; $P = 2$, $Y = 300$; $P = 3$, $Y = 267$.

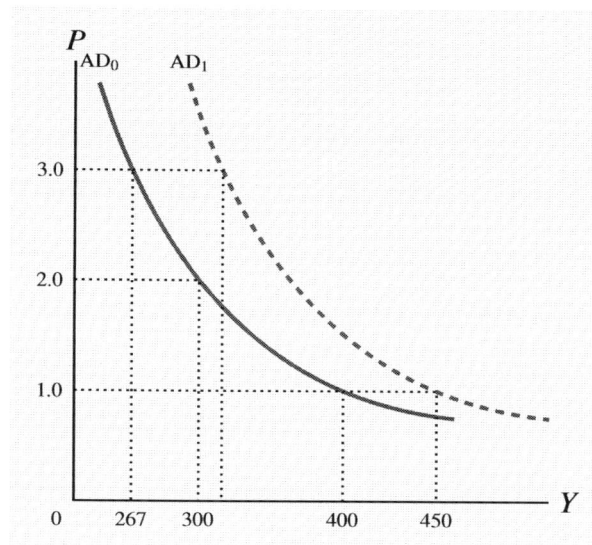

(d) The AD curve would lie everywhere to the right of AD_0 at: $P = 1$, $Y = 450$; $P = 2$, $Y = 350$; and $P = 3$, $Y = 317$, giving AD_1 in the diagram for part (c).

Exercise 11.5.

(a) The price level when real GDP is $Y = 360$ is:

$$P = 100 + 1.5(1,000/180) = 100 + 1.5(5.56) = 108.3$$

Similarly when $Y = 640$, $P = 109.4$ and when $Y = 840$, $P = 110.7$. These values give the AS curve plotted as:

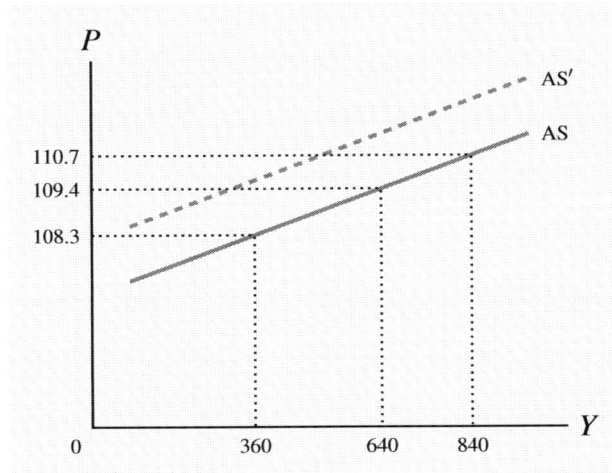

(b) Labour productivity (Y/N) decreases as output increases and, with a fixed money wage rate, raises labour cost per unit of output. Producers need higher prices to cover these higher costs if they are going to supply more output. Therefore the AS curve is upward sloping. An increase in Y involves increased costs and increased prices.

(c) When $W = 1,100$ and $Y = 360$, $P = 100 + 1.5(1,100/180) = 109.2$. Similarly with $Y = 640$, $P = 110.3$ and with $Y = 840$, $P = 111.8$.

The dotted AS′ curve illustrates the effect of an increase in the wage rate on AS.

(d) The higher money wage rate raises labour costs per unit at every level of output. Producers needed a higher price to cover this increase in costs if they are going to continue to supply the same level of output.

Exercise 11.6.

(a) The AD and AS functions are plotted as:

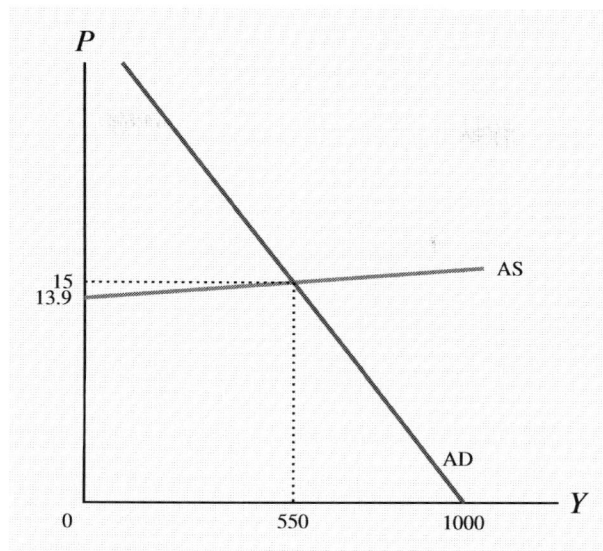

(b) Equilibrium values from AD = AS are $P = 15$, $Y = 550$.

(c) If $Y_P = 650$ there is a recessionary gap of 100.

(d) From AD = AS, equilibrium $Y = 583/1.06 = 550$. Note that the denominator of 1.06 captures the effect of the change in price along AS when any change in AE that shifts the AD curve (i.e. a change in the number 583 in this case). Closing the recessionary gap of 100 so $Y = 650$ with an increase in G, when the simple expenditure multiplier with constant prices is 2.0, calls for:

$$650 = (583 + 2\Delta G)/1.06$$
$$\Delta G = 53$$

An increase in government expenditure of 53 is required to close the gap, recognizing that the positively sloped AS curve means prices rise and offset some of the increase in expenditure as Y increases.

Exercise 11.7.

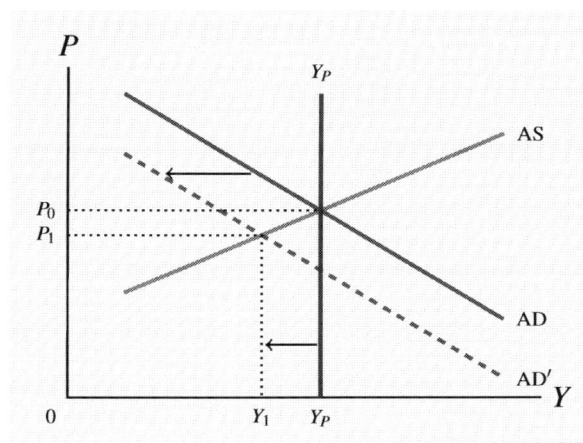

A fall in exports reduces AD by $\Delta X/(1 - \text{slope of AE})$ at every level of Y. Equilibrium Y falls from Y_P to Y_1 and lowers P from P_0 to P_1. The result is a recessionary gap equal to $Y_1 - Y_P$.

Exercise 11.8. A fall in the money wage rate will only work to reduce or eliminate a recessionary gap if lowers the AS curve without disturbing the AD curve. However, if debt contracts like loans, lines of credit, mortgages and bonds are defined in money terms, a fall in money wage rates reduces the flow of money income needed to service those contracts. Expenditures on goods and services would be reduced and some households and businesses would face insolvencies. In these circumstances the fall in wage rates reduces AD as AS falls and the equilibrium Y falls, increasing the recessionary gap.

Exercise 11.9. A rise in money wage rates would work to reduce an inflationary gap by raising production costs, shifting AS and prices upwards, raising interest rates and reducing expenditures along the AD curve until $\text{AD} = \text{AS}$ at Y_P.

Exercise 11.10. In the diagram on the left the central bank sets the monetary base at MB_0 which, given current fundamental conditions, supports $\text{AD}_{(MB_0)}$ needed for equilibrium at Y_P.

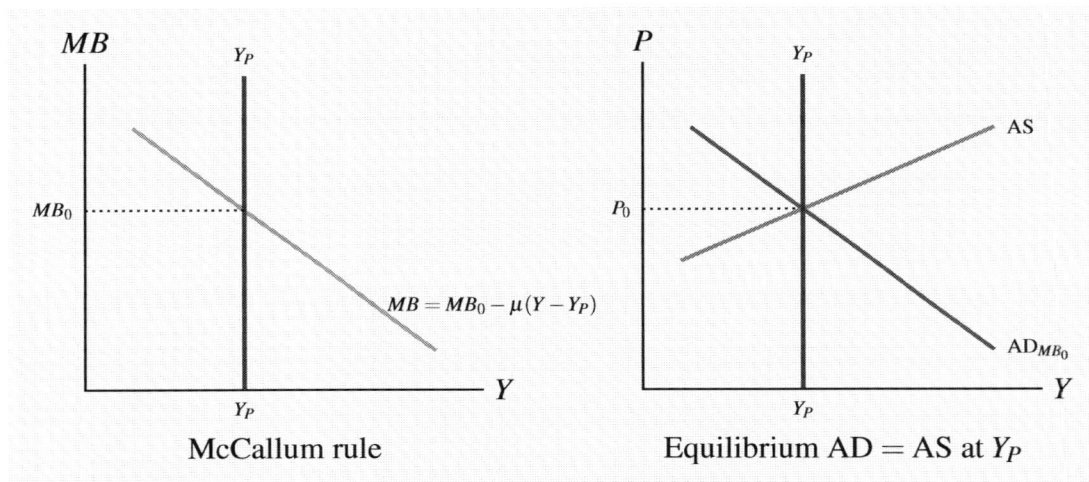

McCallum rule   Equilibrium AD = AS at Y_P

Exercise 11.11. Based on a McCallum rule, the central bank would react to transitory changes in economic conditions that shifted AD, and caused temporary departures from Y_P by changing MB as shown by movements along the MB rule. For example, the reaction to a transitory increase in AD would be a cut in MB, moving to the right and down the MB function. That would tighten credit conditions and reduce expenditure.

The central bank would react to a change in *fundamental economic conditions* by resetting its MB_0 target, which would shift the MB function and the AD curve.

Exercise 11.12.

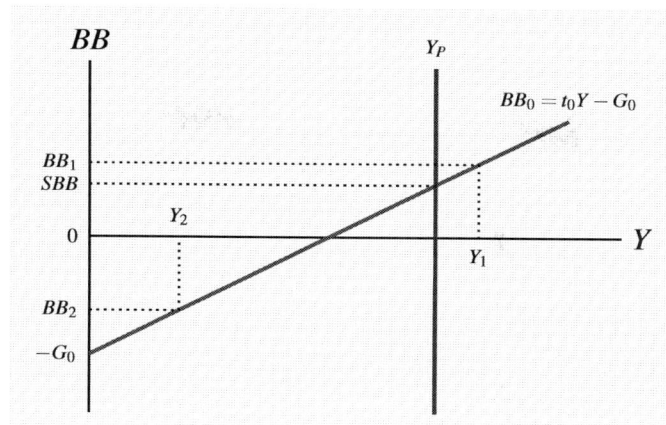

The budget function BB_0 is defined by the tax rate t_0 and expenditure G_0 set in the government's budget plan. It would produce a structural budget surplus SBB at Y_P.

If economic conditions caused either inflationary or recessionary gaps actual budget balances would be either BB_1, a larger surplus, or BB_2, a budget deficit, respectively.

Exercise 11.13. In the diagram above, the actual budget balance with an inflationary gap, $Y > Y_P$, is higher than the structural budget balance SBB.

Exercise 11.14.

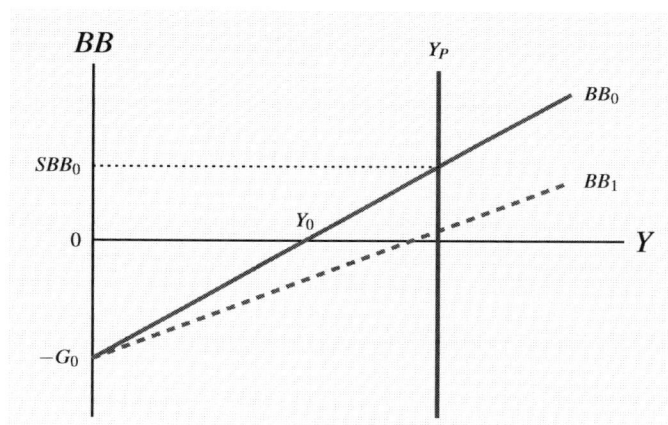

The economy is initially at Y_0 with a recessionary gap and a balanced budget $BB = 0$. Fiscal stimulus, as cut in the tax rate, shifts BB_0 to BB_1. The recessionary gap is eliminated. The structural and actual budget balances are equal with a small budget deficit.

Solutions to exercises for Chapter 12

Exercise 12.1. The equilibrium inflation rate is determined by AD and Y_P at the expected inflation π^e. An increase in export demand would shift AD to the right and raise the equilibrium inflation rate.

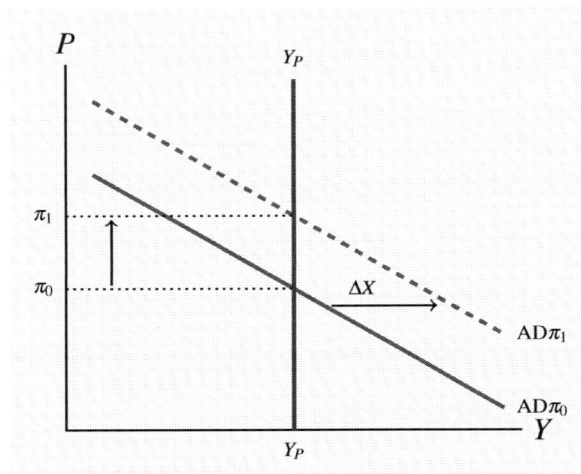

If the central bank reacted to defend its inflation target as π_0, it would raise its interest rate and money supply growth would decrease to shift AD back from AD_1 to AD_0. **Exercise 12.2.** With AD: $Y = 1,150 - 25\pi$ and $Y_P = 1,000$ the equilibrium inflation rate is:

$$1,000 = 1,150 - 25\pi$$
$$25\pi = 150$$
$$\pi = 6.0$$

This inflation rate is above the central bank's $\pi^* = 4.0$ target. The bank would have to raise its interest rate to reduce AD and lower the inflation rate to 4.0%.

Exercise 12.3. Increased investment shifts $AD\pi$ to $AD\pi_1$, increase real GDP and will put upward pressure on the inflation rate. However, as the new capital stock and technology comes on stream Y_P grows to Y_{P1}, offsetting the initial inflationary gap. The final result is a higher level of real GDP at Y_{P1} with inflation at the initial level π^*, the central bank's target.

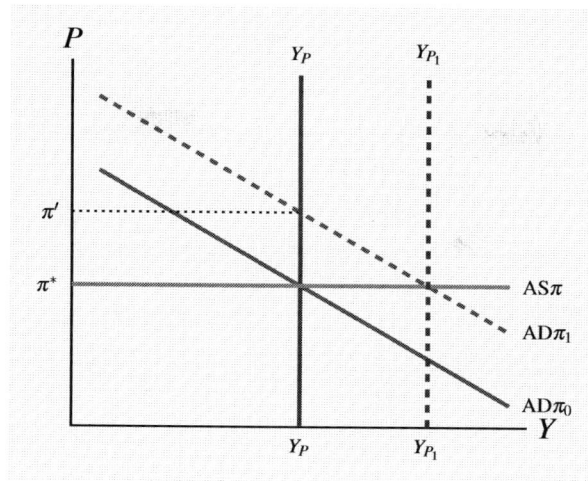

Exercise 12.4. A higher rate of increase in wages shifts AS up as the rate of increase in real costs of production rises at each level of output.

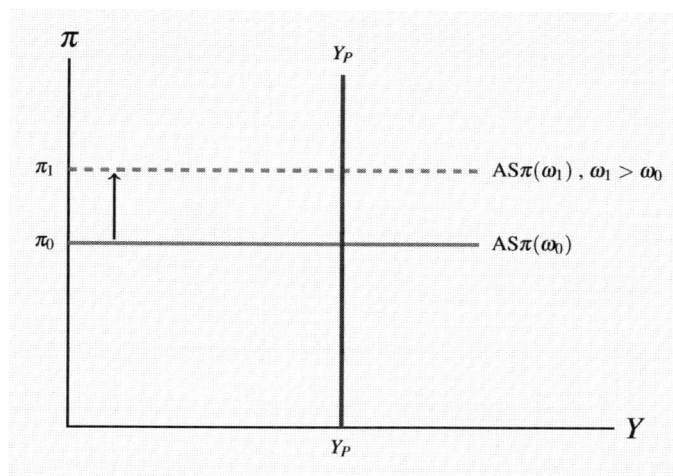

Exercise 12.5. The economy is initially in equilibrium at Y_P and π_0. A fall in exports shift $AD\pi$ left to $AD\pi_1$, opening a recessionary gap $Y_1 - Y_P$. The inflation rate is not changed in the short run but will decline over time if the recessionary gap persists.

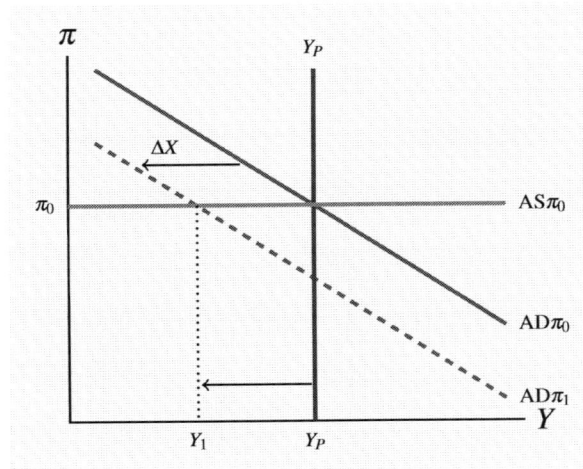

Exercise 12.6.

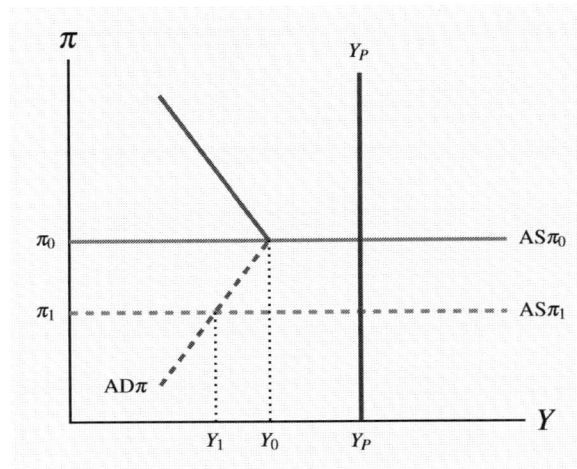

With the economy at Y_0 and the central bank having reduced its policy rate to the lower bound to fight the persistent recessionary gap, the ADπ curve has a positive slope at any inflation rate less than π_0. Any fall in the inflation rate from π_0 raises the real interest rate $(i - \pi)$ because the bank cannot counter with a lower nominal interest rate. Higher real rates reduce expenditures and output.

Furthermore, cuts in the rate of increase in money wage rates or any other cost reductions that lower the inflation rate that shift ASπ down, will increase rather than reduce the recessionary gap: e.g. $Y_1 - Y_P$ in the diagram.

Exercise 12.7.

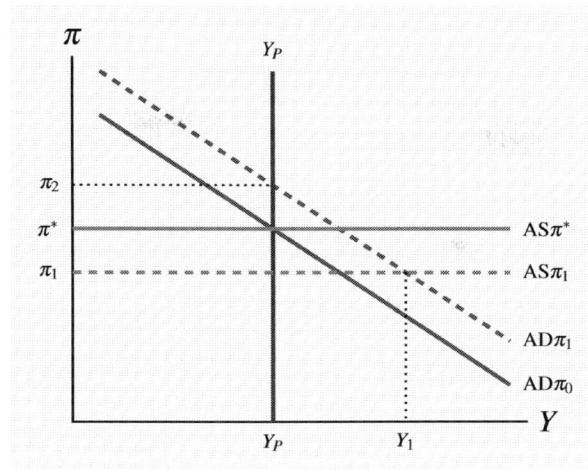

In the diagram the economy is at $\pi^* Y_P$ before the tax cut. Cutting the GST lowers ASπ to ASπ_1 and shifts AD to ADπ_1. The result is an initial fall in the inflation rate and an inflationary gap $Y_1 - Y_P$. However, ADπ_1 is too strong for long run equilibrium at the Bank's target inflation rate π^*. The Bank reacts by raising its policy interest rate to reduce ADπ to its initial value. When equilibrium is restored at π^*, Y_P households and businesses enjoy lower rates of GST on expenditures but higher interest rates on debt.

Exercise 12.8.

(a) Given that $\Delta pd = -sppb + (i-n)pd$, and the both i and n are not policy instruments, the $spbb$ required for $\Delta pd = 0$ is:

$$0 = -spbb + (i-n)pd$$
$$spbb = (i-n)pd$$

If the interest rate on the public debt is greater than the rate of growth in nominal GDP a $spbb > 0$ is required to stabilize the debt ratio. Alternatively, $n > i$ permits a primary budget deficit without increasing the debt ratio.

(b) If the rate of growth of Y falls a fiscal policy that increases in the $spbb$ is required to maintain public debt ratio.

(c) An increase in the $spbb$ reduces ADπ and reduces n, which at least partially offsets the attempt to maintain pd.

(d) A lower interest rate would increase ADπ and n and lower future i costs of carrying the public debt. The result would be a smaller $(i-n)$ in the Δpd function, supporting the government's $\Delta pd = 0$ target.

Solutions to exercises for Chapter 13

Exercise 13.1.

(a) Growth in potential GDP is growth in the capacity of the economy to produce goods and services. Growth in per capita real GDP is growth in the economy's output of goods and services per person.

(b) Growth in per capita real output is a measure of growth in the standard of living. Growth in per capita real output depends on both the growth in total real output and the growth in population.

(c) If population is growing, growth in per capita real GDP will be less than growth in potential GDP.

Exercise 13.2.

(a) Ten years in the future the country with a growth rate of 3.5% will have potential GDP of $141 billion, while the country with a growth rate of 3.25% will have potential GDP of $138 billion, a difference of 2.2 percent.

(b) Twenty years in the future the potential GDPs will be $200 billion and $190 billion respectively, a difference of 5.3 percent.

Exercise 13.3. By growth accounting the contributions to annual growth in potential output are:

(a) Labour force growth 1.4%.

(b) Capita stock growth 1.0%.

(c) Improved productivity 1.1%.

Exercise 13.4. By growth accounting the growth in real GDP = 0.7(growth in labour force) + 0.3(growth in capital stock) = 0.7(2.5) + 0.3(1.5) = 1.75 + 0.45 = 2.2%. Capital stock does not grow as fast as labour force with the result that falling labour productivity reduces output per worker.

Exercise 13.5.

(a) Annual growth in country A is 2.9% and in country B 3.9%.

(b) Country A because output growth is greater than labour force growth.

Solutions ▪ 95

(c) The capital to labour ratio rises in A but falls in B.

(d) Faster growth in total output in B comes from faster growth in the labour force but the fall in the capital to labour ratio in B lowers labour productivity, which is output per worker.

Exercise 13.6. With equal growth rates of capital and labour at 2.5% a year, the capital/labour ratio is constant and the economy enjoys constant returns to scale. Potential output will grow at 2.5% a year.

Per capita output will be constant as output and labour grow at the same rate.

Improved technology that increased total factor productivity by 1.5% a year would result in growth in per capita real GDP by 2.5% a year.

Exercise 13.7.

(a) Technology is the key to improved standards of living because increases in output per worker arising from increases in the capital to labour ratio are limited by diminishing returns and eventually fall to zero.

(b) Increasing capital per worker $(K/N = k)$ move the economy along the per worker output function with a decreasing slope caused by diminishing returns to the capital per worker ratio. Increase in k from k_0 to k_2 result in smaller and smaller increase in y.

(c) An improvement in productivity (ΔA) shifts the production function up, raising y at every k and is not subject to diminishing returns. In the diagram, improved productivity increases y from y_2 to y_4 without any change in labour or capital inputs. Productivity growth from new technology has the potential to provide sustained increases in output per worker and standards of living.

Exercise 13.8.

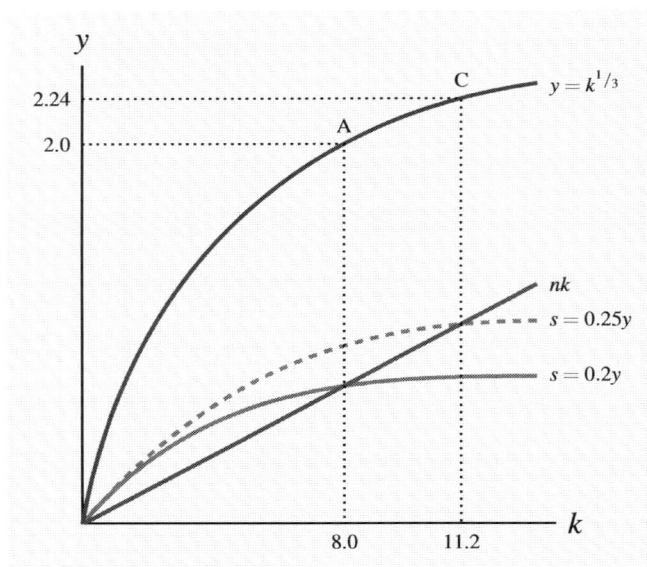

(a) The steady state level of output per worker is 2.

(b) The rate of growth of total GDP is 5% (0.05).

(c) If savings were $0.25y$ the steady state output per worker would be 2.24.

(d) The rate of growth of total output in this new steady state would be 5% (0.05).

(e) Points A and C show the steady state outputs per worker based on parts (a) and (c).

Exercise 13.9.

(a) The convergence hypothesis argues that countries with the same technology, population growth and savings rates will move to (converge on) the same level of steady state output per worker.

(b) OECD countries with lower per capita income are operating below their steady state per capita income and thus must grow faster than higher income countries to arrive at the same steady state per capita income levels.

(c) No. Poor African countries may have a different set of basic conditions, for example higher rates of population growth, lower savings rates and inferior technology, which result in a steady state per capita income less than that of the industrialized countries.

Solutions to exercises for Chapter 14

Exercise 14.1.

(a) The balance of payments is always zero, neither deficit nor surplus. Any deficit or surplus on current account that is not offset by a surplus or deficit on capital account results in a change in official reserve holdings, and a corresponding entry to balance the balance of payments account. The current account balance, the capital account balance and the change in official reserves sum to zero.

(b) Official reserves would increase by $2 billion, the difference between the surplus on current account and the deficit on capital account.

(c) The central bank would buy foreign currency to add to the official reserve account.

(d) The monetary base increases. The central bank pays for the foreign currency it buys by issuing new central bank deposits, which are monetary base.

Exercise 14.2. The US experienced the higher inflation rate as prices doubled over 10 years while Canadian prices increase by 75%. A nominal exchange rate of $1.05 CDN for $1.00US would preserve the real exchange rate. The Canadian dollar appreciated in terms of US dollars and the US dollar depreciated in terms of Canadian dollars.

Exercise 14.3. The purchase of US government securities by Canadian portfolio managers is an import of securities. Payment for these securities is made to residents of other countries and capital flows out from Canada to other countries. The capital account balance in the balance of payments is reduced.

Exercise 14.4. The nominal interest rate in Canada by 1 percent higher than that in the US reflects, and an expected rate of appreciation of 1 percent in the US dollar, if interest rate parity prevails.

Exercise 14.5. The 'interest parity condition' occurs when differences in interest rates between countries are matched by the expectation that changes in exchange rates will offset interest rate differences and result in equal returns from holding assets denominated in different national currencies. If interest rates in Canada are higher than those in the US the interest parity condition predicts a fall in the international value of the Canadian dollar. The fall in the Canadian dollar results in a loss on the exchange rate transaction involved in buying and subsequently selling assets denominated in foreign currencies.

Exercise 14.6.

Cdn $/US $

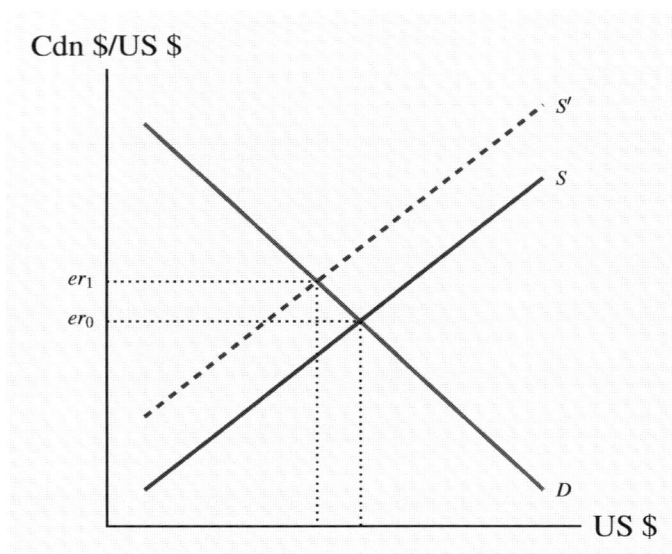

A sharp and persistent drop in natural gas and crude oil prices would lower Canadian export receipts and the supply of US dollars on the foreign exchange market. The Canadian exchange rate would rise as the Canadian dollar depreciated.

Exercise 14.7.

(a) The demand for foreign exchange (US dollars) in the diagram comes from Canadian demand for imports of foreign goods and services on the current account and foreign financial assets on the capital account. The demand for goods and services comes from Canadian incomes and tastes in terms of the propensity to import and the real exchange rate. The demand for foreign assets comes from Canadian portfolio decisions to hold foreign assets based on interest rate differentials and expected returns.

Cdn $ price of US $

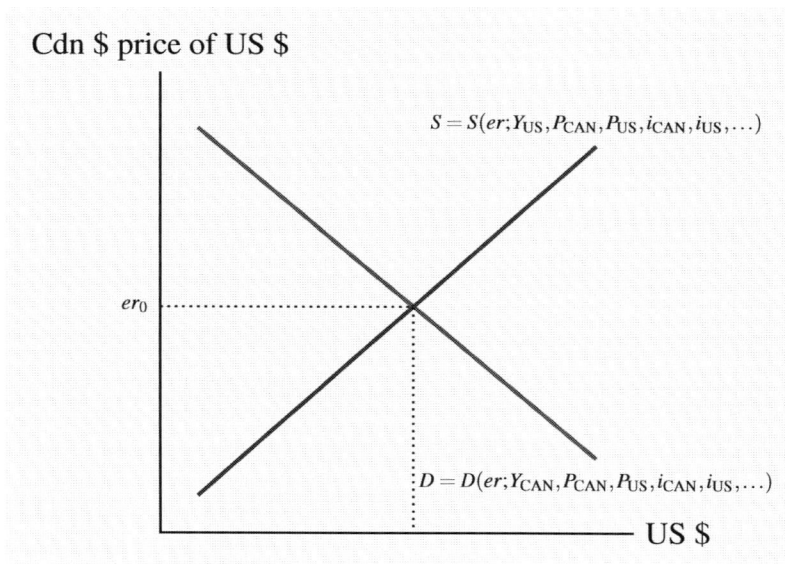

(b) The supply of foreign exchange (US dollars) comes from foreign demand for Canadian goods, services and assets based on foreign incomes and tastes, the real exchange rate, interest rate differentials and expected returns.

(c) The equilibrium exchange rate er_0 is the exchange rate at which the balances on current account and capital account sum to zero.

Exercise 14.8.

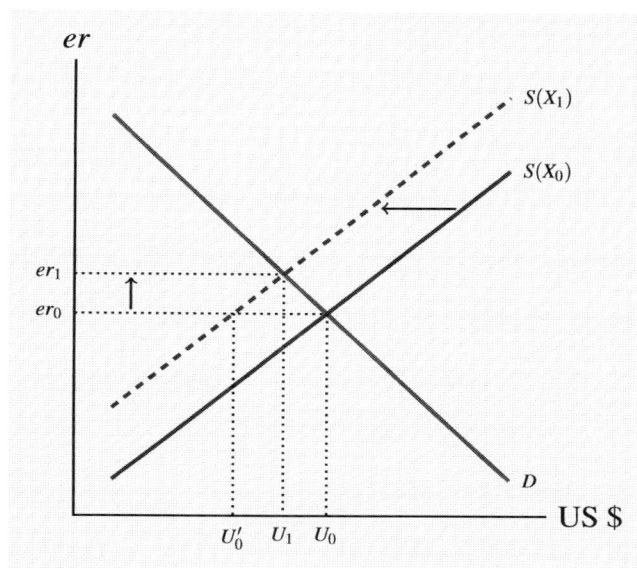

(a) With a flexible exchange rate the fall in exports reduces the current account balance and the supply of foreign exchange derived from export receipts. The supply curve $S(X_0)$ shifts to the left to $S(X_1)$. The exchange rate rises from er_0 to er_1 to maintain equilibrium in the balance of payments.

(b) If there were no change in the exchange rate the fall in exports would reduce the supply of foreign exchange to U_0' and create a corresponding deficit on current account. With flexible rates, the rise in the exchange rate raises the domestic price of imports and increases the profitability and competitiveness of exports. The quantity of foreign exchange demanded to finance imports is reduced while the supply of foreign exchange from exports is increased to establish equilibrium at er_1 and U_1.

(c) With flexible rates the foreign exchange market adjusts without intervention and there is no change in official reserve holdings.

Exercise 14.9.

(a) Fixed exchange rate (er^*):

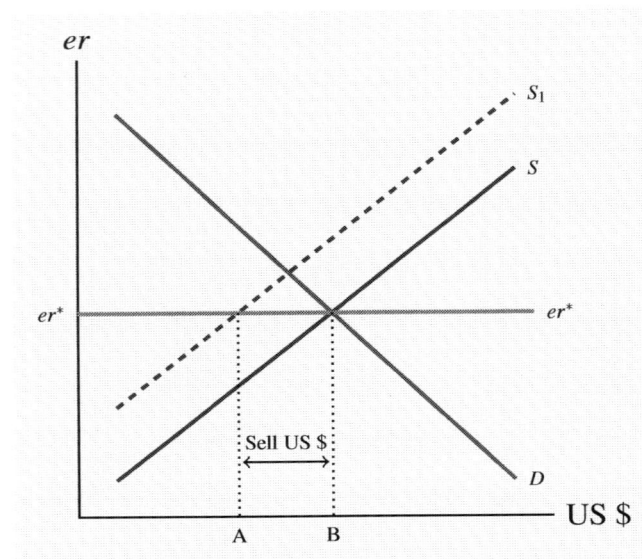

(b) The decline in exports reduces the balance on the current account in the balance of payments and reduces the supply of foreign exchange in the foreign exchange market. In the diagram the decline in the current account balance, measured in US dollars is $U_0 - U_1$, ($= er^* \times (U_0 - U_1)$ in Cdn \$). The supply curve shifts to the left by this amount.

(c) To defend the fixed exchange rate at er^* the central bank sells foreign exchange from the official reserve account equal to the AB in the diagram, the difference between market supply and demand at the fixed rate er^*.

(d) The central bank sale of US \$ would reduce holdings of official reserves and the monetary base.

Exercise 14.10. Flexible exchange rates provide for two linkages in the transmission mechanism for monetary policy. Changes in interest rates in pursuit of short-term stabilization objectives produce complementary changes in the exchange rate. Higher interest rates cause an appreciation of the domestic currency and lower interest rates depreciation. Monetary policy has simultaneous effects on domestic expenditures and net exports. By contrast, with flexible exchange rates and a monetary policy that controls money supply, fiscal policy is weakened by both interest rate and exchange rate crowding out. Fiscal expansion raises income and the demand for money pushing interest rates up and lowering the exchange rate with the result that investment and net exports are reduced.

Exercise 14.11. With a fixed exchange rate policy, interest rates must be maintained at the level required by the fixed exchange rate. Expansionary fiscal policies that raise real GDP and the demand for money must be matched by an expansion in the money supply to keep interest rates from rising. As a result crowding out does not impair the power of fiscal policy as it would in a closed economy or in an open economy with flexible exchange rates.

Solutions to exercises for Chapter 15

Exercise 15.1.

(a) Northland has an absolute advantage in the production of both goods, as it has lower labour requirements for each.

(b) The opportunity cost of 1 bushel of wheat is 1/2 litre of wine in Northland and 3/4 litre of wine in Southland.

(c) Northland has a comparative advantage in wheat while Southland does in wine.

(d) By reducing wheat production by 1 bushel, Southland can produce an additional 3/4 litre of wine.

(e) Both countries can gain if Northland shifts production from wine to wheat and the countries trade wine for wheat at a rate between 1/2 litre of wine for 1 bushel of wheat and 3/4 litre of wine for one bushel of wheat.

(f) By reducing wine production by 1/2 litre, Northland can increase wheat production by 1 bushel, which, at Southland's opportunity cost, exchanges for 3/4 litre of wine, giving Northland a gain of 1/4 litre of wine.

Exercise 15.2.

(a) The US has an absolute advantage in both goods.

(b) Canada has a comparative advantage in xylophones. The US has a comparative advantage in yogourt.

(c) See diagram below.

(d) See diagram below.

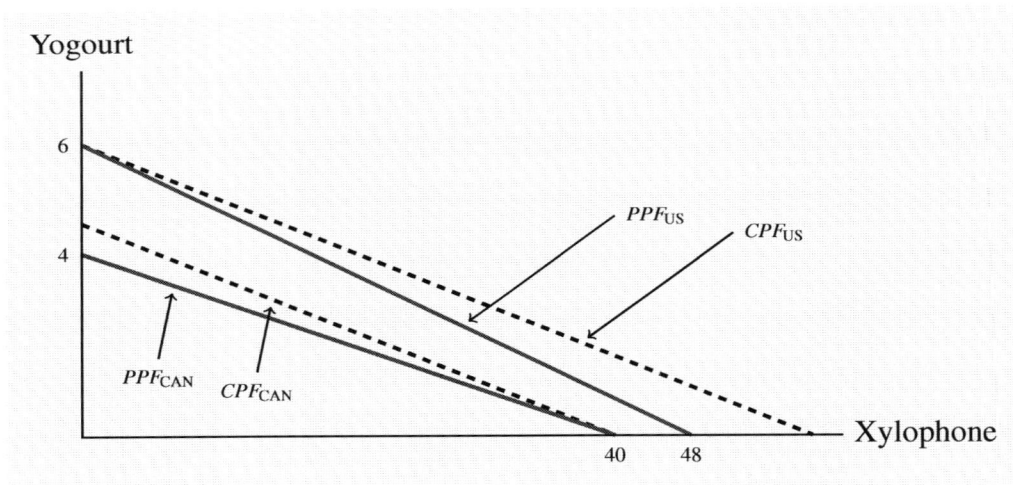

Exercise 15.3.

(a) The diagram shows that the amount traded is 60 units; of which domestic producers supply 5 and 55 are imported.

(b) In this case, the foreign supply curve SW shifts up from a price of $18 to $24. The amount traded is now 40 units, 20 of which are supplied domestically.

(c) Tariff revenue is EFHI= $120.

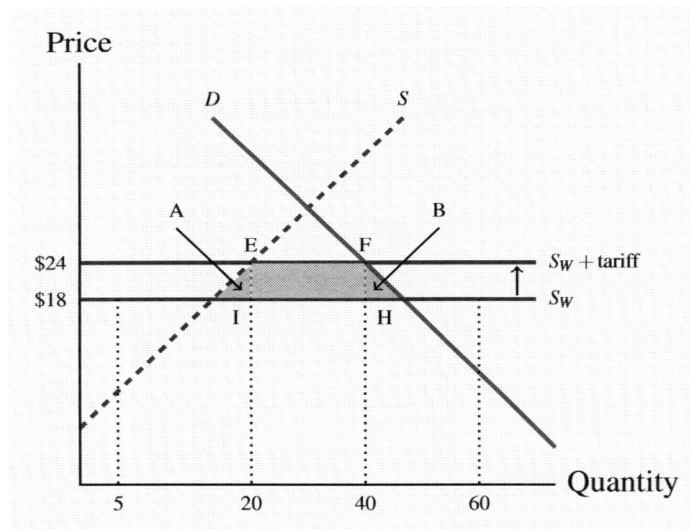

Exercise 15.4.

(a) The deadweight losses correspond to the two triangles, A and B, in the diagram, and amount to $105.

(b) The amount of additional profit for domestic producers is $75.

Exercise 15.5.

(a) See figure below.

(b) The total quantity of trade is 100 units, of which 80 are supplied domestically.

(c) The subsidy shifts the domestic supply curve down by $2 at each quantity. This supply intersects the demand curve at $Q = 100$. Foreign producers are squeezed out of the market completely.

(d) Cost to the government is $200.

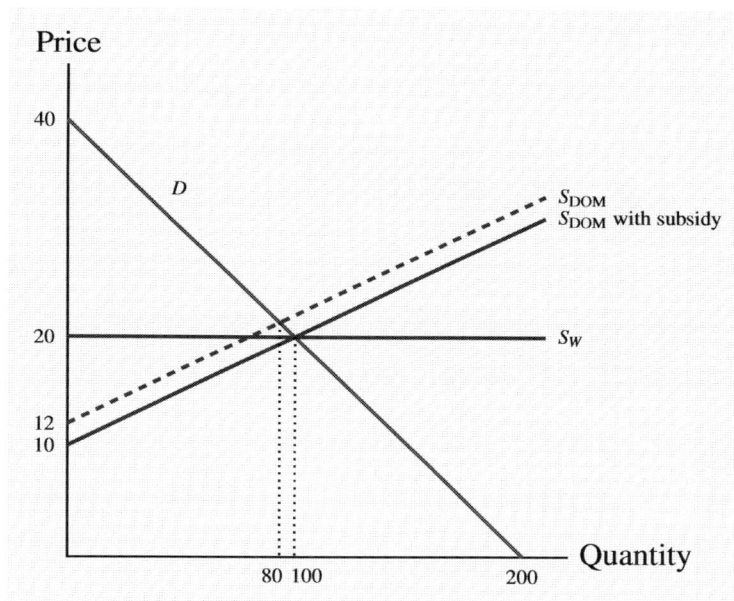

Exercise 15.6.

(a) See diagram below.

(b) Domestic producers will supply 80 and imports will be 112.

(c) The equilibrium with the quota is point A in the diagram with imports equal to the quota of 76.

(d) The equilibrium quantity with the quota is 180, with 76 imported and 104 supplied by domestic producers. The equilibrium market price is $38.

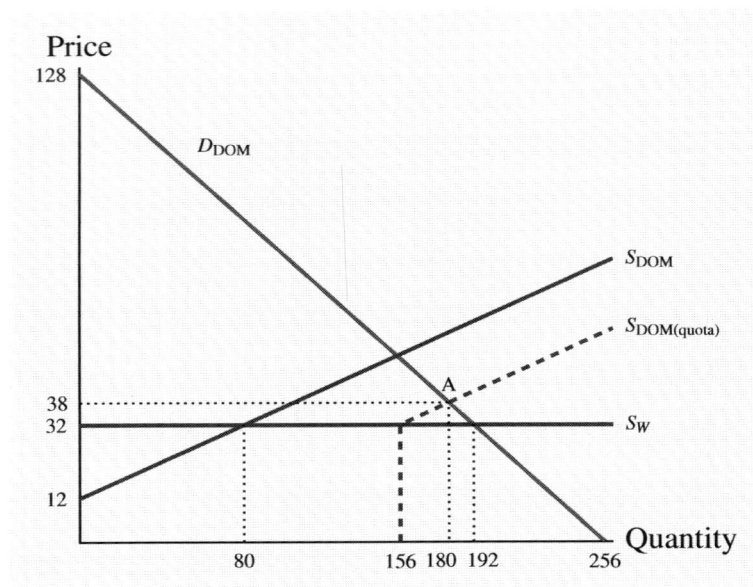

Exercise 15.7.

(a) See diagram below.

(b) See diagram below.

(c) The quantity permitted to be brought to market would be 40 units, even though the supply side would be willing to supply more at this price, buyers will demand just 40 at a price of $28.

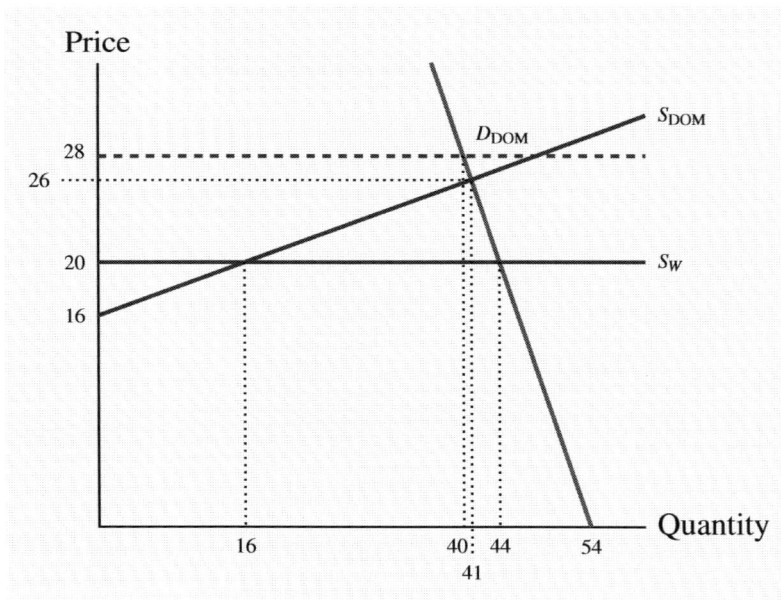

Exercise 15.8. The figure below illustrates parts (a) through (f). Since the total production before trade was 20 of each, and after specialization it is 30 of each, the gain is 10 of each good.

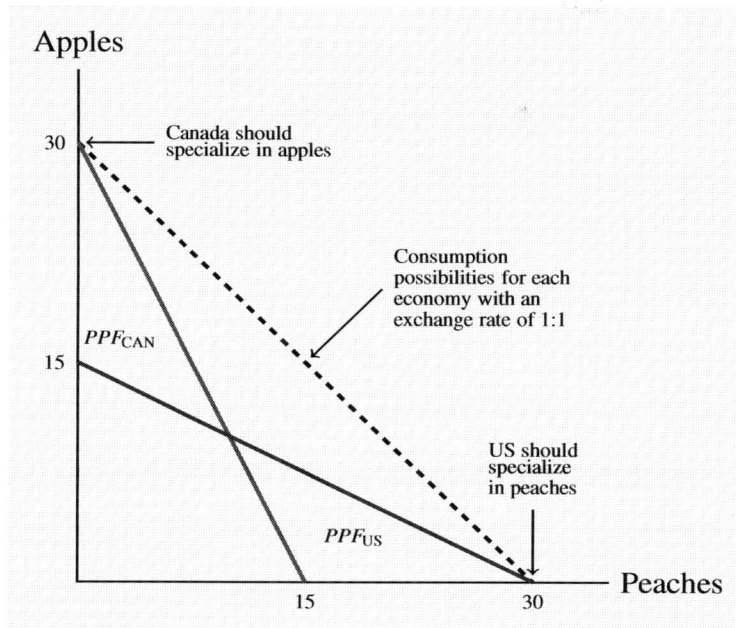

Printed in Great Britain
by Amazon